⮢ The Other People ⮠

Sea View wasn't at all as Kate imagined; neither was Aunt Poppy. Instead of a smart hotel Kate found an ordinary guest house run by an aunt quite unlike the elegant relative she'd expected, and an extraordinary collection of other people. Yet it was they who largely contributed to the success of Kate's holiday, their lives and relationships absorbing her more fully than any of the pleasures she'd anticipated, like the sun, the beach and the moonlit sea.

The Other People

by Janet McNeill

CHATTO & WINDUS

LONDON

First published in 1970 by
Little, Brown and Company
Boston and Toronto

First published in Great Britain 1972 by
Chatto & Windus Ltd
40–42 William IV Street
London WC2N 4DF

Second Impression 1974

ISBN 0 7011 0494 5

Reproduced and printed in Great Britain by
Lowe & Brydone (Printers) Ltd., Thetford, Norfolk

The Other People

◁(I)▷

SHE FOLLOWED her aunt up the stairs, noticing small things to avoid thinking about larger ones. Aunt Poppy's ankles were thick. So were her stockings. The stair carpet was pink with green leaves and sprays of blue flowers. Some of the flowers were worn away so that the white canvas threads of the carpet showed through like fish-bones. On the second landing Aunt Poppy opened a door and stood aside, allowing Kate to go in first. "This is your room," she said, "next door to mine. I hope you're going to be very happy here, child."

Kate went into the room and stood without turning round. "Thank you, Aunt Poppy, it's a very nice room," she said. She was glad she had her back to her aunt because she needed to squeeze the words out, the way you squeeze toothpaste when the tube is almost finished. She didn't want Aunt Poppy to guess that what she really meant was, "This is terrible. I didn't think it would be like this."

Aunt Poppy said, "I expect you're tired after your journey. You must have been up very early this morning."

"It was early." Kate couldn't remember much about the start of the journey now that she had come to the

3

end of it. The day stretched back to a morning that was already years and years away. There was nothing inside her head now except floating cotton wool and a procession of fields and hedges running away in the other direction, the pattern that the sound of the train had left behind and the faces of the passengers in the carriage, all of them carrying a private world behind their eyes. Anyway, she didn't want to think too hard about home in case the realness of it got muddled up with the strangeness of this place. For a panicky moment she tried to remember the pattern on the stair carpet at home and found she couldn't. What did it matter now, anyway? And yet it did matter.

"You're going to feel at home with us, aren't you? We're just one happy family here at Sea View," Aunt Poppy said. She sounded anxious that this addition to the family might be a misfit. Good, thought Kate, that makes two of us. "It was very kind of you to have me," she said firmly and heard a small sigh from the doorway where her aunt was standing.

"Your mother got a good day, didn't she?"

"Yes. It was fine."

"Paris, that's where they're going, isn't it?"

"Yes."

"Her first visit, is it?"

"Yes."

"You must send her a letter straightaway, mustn't you, to tell her you arrived here safe and sound. You've got her address, haven't you?"

"Yes."

There was a silence during which the smell of frying fish came in through the open window.

"Well now," Aunt Poppy said, "I'll leave you to settle in, shall I? There are hangers in the wardrobe and the bathroom is the door at the end of the passage. You'll hear the bell for high tea. Don't be late, will you, dear? I always ask our guests to try to be punctual. And if there's anything you want you'll just mention it, won't you?"

Kate wondered what would happen if she said, "I want to go home!"— if she said it out loud, rudely, like a red-faced child, so that the words bounced back off the walls and nobody could help hearing.

"My, you've grown, haven't you?" Aunt Poppy declared. "Shot up quite a lot since the last photograph your mother sent me."

"I was thirteen in June."

"So you were! Just imagine!" Aunt Poppy said this as if very few people were clever enough to be thirteen at any time, let alone in June. Unless I'm careful, Kate thought, she will be bringing me hot milk and biscuits and tucking me in with a teddy bear and a bedtime story. That would be a laugh. What was it about relatives that seemed to push you back into bibs and short socks? She wished her aunt would go away and leave her so that she could grow into her proper age and size again. What would Hazel think if she could see her now? Hazel had been thirteen in May. With the money her grannie had given her she bought a pair of false eyelashes. Fabulous, she looked. When she wasn't wearing them she kept them in a little glass tube with a stopper, like a couple of hairy caterpillars off duty.

From the hall two flights below a clock cleared its throat and began to strike the hour. It was a showy, high-pitched strike, with a lot of whirr beforehand.

"High tea is at half-past," Aunt Poppy said. "I must go and see how things are coming along in the kitchen; we've got a full house just now." She twisted up some tails of hair that had come loose on her forehead and tucked the ends in any old way. "Come down when you're ready," she said.

Kate waited for the door to close but her aunt spoke again. "When you lean a little way out of your window and look over to the right you can see the sea," she urged.

If she's waiting for me to make a mad rush over to the window and gasp then she'll have to wait, Kate decided, standing where she was. It was Stout Cortez who gasped, not Kate Lucas.

Aunt Poppy said, "It's a beautiful beach."

"I know, Aunt Poppy. You sent us postcards."

"There are two other girls staying here, a little older than you perhaps but it will be nice for you to have someone to go about with, won't it?"

"Yes."

"Well — bye-bye for now, then." At last the door had closed. The sound of Aunt Poppy's feet travelling down the pink stair carpet grew fainter and disappeared.

Kate went to the window and leaned out, looking first

to the left, on purpose. Her room was at the back of the house. The building on the left was set farther from the road so that Kate had a good view of it. Red neon letters proclaimed it to be the Hotel Splendide. Neon letters shining in the middle of the afternoon have an expensive festive appearance. Very smart and smooth the hotel looked, very classy. Splendide was right. There were striped umbrellas in the garden and white tables, borders of flowers, and colonies of storks and gnomes. A boy in a white jacket was gathering glasses from the tables, wiping the tables with a cloth. A red sports car posed glossily on the gravel. Two girls in bikinis lay outstretched on the grass, soaking up sun like blotting paper, the way people do in advertisements. Probably on the other side of the Hotel Splendide the grounds extended right down to the beach. The girls in the bikinis, when they had toasted themselves to a pleasing ripeness, would get up and run straight into the waves, all brown and beautiful, with their hair floating out behind them.

No chance of doing anything like that from the grounds of Sea View Guest House (Proprietor Miss Poppy Lucas — Personal Attention — Every Home Comfort). Grounds? The front of the guest house was right on the street, and behind it a high-walled strip just as wide as the house itself, with a low tangle of greenery visible beyond the flutter of tea towels which decorated the clothes-lines in the bin-studded yard. There was no direct way down to the beach. How could there be with that other house between Sea View and the sea?

It was a shabby old house, low and long, not a gleam from the dirty windows or the salt-bleached paint. Last year's leaves packed its gutters, grass sprouted from the chimney pots. Shrubs that had grown for years unhindered smothered the lower windows; a rose bush had pushed long spiked arms against the upper sills and was flaunting three enormous blooms, to show the gardening experts they were wrong. Across every window, though it was only late afternoon and August, a curtain was drawn, giving the appearance of a row of closed eyelids. Some of the curtains had not been wide enough and had been brought together and pinned. The blind house, Kate thought. It isn't interested in any view.

She turned at last to the right and leaned far out. There it was, beyond the blind house, a small tame dark blue patch that could only be the sea, six whole inches of it before the tin roof of a garage got in the way. So much then was true. Sea View Guest House had earned its title.

That was all it had earned. No marks for anything else. Kate turned away from the window and slumped on the bed — a different kind of springiness from the springiness of her own bed at home. Disappointment choked her. She could cry now if she wanted to, but she was too cross and crying was too much bother.

It was all so different from the way she had imagined it. It wasn't going to be like this at all. She remembered breaking the glad tidings to Hazel a couple of weeks past, when they were on their way home from school. She'd done it cleverly, keeping it casual on purpose.

"Oh, did I tell you — I'm going to stay with my aunt in August. She has a hotel at Sunny Bay."

"You mean your mum isn't going with you?"

This was a little tricky. "No. We're going on separate holidays this year."

"You mean your aunt owns a hotel?" The news had had its effect, Hazel was impressed, you could tell by the funny way her nose twitched.

"Oh, didn't I ever tell you?" Visions of revolving doors and a lounge with chairs as big and lush as South Sea Islands. Visions of Aunt Poppy in a smart silky dress with pearls round her neck and varnished fingernails, sitting in her office in the mornings doing accounts and seeing whether the flowers the florist had sent for the tables in the dining-room were the ones she had ordered.

"Close to the sea, is it?"

"Right slap on the Promenade." Visions of herself like Venus, only going into the water as well as coming out.

"What's it like, Sunny Bay?"

"I haven't been before but she sent us postcards. A whopping great pier. And I'll be there for the fireworks display." The exciting smell of gunpowder, and the summer sky netted with coloured light.

"Dancing, I suppose. I expect they get the good groups."

"Bound to — a place like Sunny Bay." A moon low over water and the sound of laughter and music. "And acres and acres of sand."

Hazel snorted and said, "You'd better watch it! You get as red as a beetroot if the sun blinks."

"Not this time I won't," Kate said smoothly. "I've bought some Bronze Bloom."

Seventeen and a half pence the bottle of Bronze Bloom had cost her, though it was no bigger than the smallest size of aspirin. It smelled like the Arabian Nights and looked like thick cold tea. "Smooth it on moments before you greet the sun," the label said. "See how Bronze Bloom caresses you and stirs the natural glow in the skin." If it hasn't spilled in your pocket by the time you've done the trek to the beach, Kate thought now, envying those girls at the Hotel Splendide.

"It'll be late dinner, I suppose?" Hazel had asked. The question didn't seem worth the trouble of an answer. What else would it be? "Funny, you never staying there before, when it was your aunt." Kate dodged a reply to this because in her heart she agreed that it was funny. Some time she'd have to tell Hazel about Mum, and Hazel might think that was funny too, but keep it quiet, Mum had said, that's the way we want it, let people know when it's over. So now Kate said, "You're going away with the family the way you always do, are you?" and Hazel said yes, she was, and it made her scream, just thinking of that caravan and the powdered milk and sardines and Happy Families or Scrabble when it rained.

Kate felt like screaming now, but screaming would do her no good. She hung up the little gold mini-dress in the wardrobe. She had planned to wear it to dinner on the evening of her arrival at Sunny Bay. She was going to slink down the stairs in it, and when the waiter had bowed her to her table she knew just how she would study the menu, keeping her eyes glued on it while the eyes of all the other people in Aunt Poppy's hotel were glued on her. High tea and fried fish didn't demand either the mini-dress or her performance. Jeans and a jersey was what this place deserved.

The wardrobe was as roomy as a bicycle shed and smelled peculiar — stale mothballs and summer after summer of other people's clothes. There was a mirror mounted on the heavy door, which creaked as she pushed it shut. Then she unpacked the beach clothes, the feather bedroom slippers, the new sponge-bag, the cosmetics (this was the first time she had possessed four kinds of eye-shadow at once, but the sight of them did nothing to cheer her now).

The wardrobe door — she hadn't closed it securely — swung open again, groaning, and in its mirror the whole room lurched alarmingly past, silvery and crooked. This time Kate made sure that the catch was properly fastened and avoided looking at her reflection in case it might tell her she was scared.

She couldn't stay in this room all evening being sorry for herself. And sooner or later she must go in search of the bathroom. The door at the end of the landing, Aunt Poppy had said. Was that what she had said? The door on the right at the end of the landing? The door on the left? And when she found it, might there not be someone else inside?

At least there was no one at all on the large square landing when she emerged. None of the doors had labels or numbers. Kate thought of discreetly named, pink-basined Powder Rooms with carpets and boxes of tissues and triple mirrors. What had Aunt Poppy really said? Left? Right? There must be some way of knowing. The doors looked at her but told her nothing.

Somewhere not far away someone was playing a recorder very softly and sweetly. It was rather a homesick little tune — you mustn't think about it in case it hooked itself on. Which door was it coming from? The sound was too indefinite to afford a clue. Behind another door people were talking with some heat but not loudly enough for Kate to hear the words. There was no hopeful guggle of taps coming from anywhere. Kate felt desperate, tempted to run up and down the landing banging on all the doors, demanding "Which is the bathroom?" from each of the astonished heads that answered.

She chose the door, gripped the handle and turned it gently. So far so good. At least it wasn't locked. She pushed it a few inches open, saw an area of flowery eiderdown spread over the bottom of a bed, and froze. The notes of the recorder slowed, then stopped like a question mark left in mid-air. In the open space a foot and ankle appeared clad in yellow socks with red tadpoles. The foot pawed at the air, caught the edge of the door, closed it firmly. Kate felt her face flame. All right, that was one door less.

Now a door across the passage had opened. A boy in jeans and sweater stood looking back into the room. Voices from inside it were directed at him.

"Well of course he wants to — don't you, Richard?" a woman's voice inquired.

A man said, "Stop telling the boy what he wants. He knows what he wants."

"What does he want, then?"

"What do you want, Richard? The pictures, or a climb up the cliffs?"

The boy said nothing, just shrugged and closed the door and wheeled round, almost bumping into Kate. "When you've finished snooping," he said, staring rudely, and went past her, rattling his way down the stairs.

All right, Kate decided, I'll start at the next door and try them all, one after another. She seized a handle and turned it boldly. The door was locked. From within a voice cried "Righty-ho, then! Hang on — won't be two shakes of a lamb's tail!"

In a moment the key turned and the door opened, breathing out a damp bathroom air. A small birdlike lady emerged, brightly brandishing her towel. "Holding up the traffic, am I?" she asked brightly. "That won't do, will it?"

Kate growled "I was just looking for the bathroom."

"And you found it!" the lady cried. "Life's always so so much easier when we know where it is, don't you think? And you must be Kate — well, that's nice, isn't it? We've been expecting you. My nieces are dying to meet you, Rose and Marni, sweet girls, you'll love them. My name's Dilys Darlington but just call me Aunt Dilly, the same as the girls do. You'll promise me that, won't you?"

"If you like."

"That's settled then," Aunt Dilly said, waving her towel in the air as if she was about to break out into a scarf dance. "See you later! Fried fish waits for no man — well, you wouldn't really expect it to, would you?" and she skipped off down the passage.

The bathroom was pitch pine and linoleum with brass taps. It was crammed full with other people's belongings. From a rail hung whole congregations of stockings, thin, pinky-brown and silky as the skins of onions. There was a huddle of damp smalls. On a shelf by themselves a whole battery of pills and medicines was drawn up. A rippled length of seaweed swung from a hook. The window had been propped a few inches open with a tin of talcum powder. There was an assorted assembly of toothpastes and toothbrushes.

Kate washed quickly, trying not to touch anything. Everything belonged to somebody else, to people she didn't know. She felt as if she were staring in at windows where she had no business. Whose were the shells in the jam pot, the pair of dumb-bells parked on the top of the cupboard? Who owned the tin of slimming biscuits? Who needed a hot water bottle in a pink velvet cover in weather like this? Her own face, reflected and distorted in the taps, looked a long way off and vaguely comical. Terror seized Kate — before she was finished, the handle of the bathroom door would turn and someone would rattle it. Would she pretend she didn't hear, or would she call "Righty-ho then!" What were the rules of this place? Was it all going to be as difficult as this?

She had forgotten to bring a towel with her and when she had finished washing she had to charge, dripping, across the landing towards the sanctuary of her own room. Halfway there, eyes screwed up to keep the water out, she cannoned into someone and felt her shoulders gripped. "Whoops! Don't forget to sound your horn," a man's voice said before the hands released her. She sped on, seeing nothing except a glimpse of a yellow tie with red tadpoles. Mad, mad as a hatter!

Safe in her own room again — for a scalding moment she hadn't been sure if it was her room — she sat on the bed and let mortification ride right up her face and into the roots of her hair. With all her heart she wished she hadn't come. Three weeks of this was ahead of her — three whole weeks, living in this house elbow to elbow with a lot of strange people, bumping into them from breakfast to supper, every visit to the bathroom a perilous excursion. She wouldn't be able to stand it.

She rummaged for her purse and felt for the return half of her ticket. She held it in her hand. The little square of cardboard comforted her, as if it had been a miniature magic carpet. She didn't have to stay. She put the ticket back in its place and went to the window and looked out, plotting an escape route. Out over the window-sill, a quick scramble to the low roof of the kitchen which extended into the yard, a foothold on the top of one of the rubbish bins — then what? A leap down into the yard, then a plunge into the tangle of untidy bushes beyond the clothes-lines. There must be some way out over the wall beyond. But even if she could climb the wall, that would only land her in the desolate garden of the blind house. On top of this came the realization that this wouldn't be any help anyway. Even if she did reach the railway station and there was a train and no one saw her or ran after her and stopped her, and even if the train was going in the right direction, there would be no one at home when she arrived. The house would be just the way it had been when the door had been slammed before she had begun her journey.

Soon she would have to go downstairs and look for the dining-room. She wished there was a place where she could go and be private, some secret solitude where she could draw the curtains on herself, and if they didn't meet could pin them, like the curtains of the blind house. She remembered other retreats, the back of the sofa where she could lie hidden long after bedtime, the bottom of the sharp-smelling shrubbery, the old bike shed at school where the kindergarten kept their rabbits.

The letters of the Hotel Splendide glowed brighter and firmer now in the summer evening, like the lights from some Promised Land. She could hear the thin throb of music from open French windows. That was what she'd thought it would be like.

All right, then, that was what she'd pretend it *was* like! She felt fierce and altogether splendid as she took the gold mini-dress out of the wardrobe without even a qualm and put it on, challenging her own reflection. She sat at the dressing-table and opened the new jars of cosmetics and did the right things to her face in the right order. She put perfume on the pulses of her wrists the way the magazine said she should — the pulses were beating like stamping grasshoppers. She looked at each of the four kinds of eye-shadow in turn and chose the green. It was called Tendresse des Arbres; she plastered a whole shrubbery of it on each of her lids.

Now feeling so unlike herself that it didn't really matter, Kate waited until the bell sounded in the hall, then opened her door and came down the stairs to meet the other people — the Mad Hatter who played the recorder and wore yellow socks with red tadpoles and a tie to match, the cross boy who couldn't make up his mind between the cliff walk and the pictures, the consumer of the slimming biscuits, the owner of the pink velvet-covered hot-water bottle, "Aunt Dilly" and her two nieces who were dying to met the new arrival at Sea View. All right then. Here she was!

～(2)～

THE GUESTS at Sea View Guest House were distributed
along a single table in the dining-room. Kate's place was
between the two nieces — if they'd been all that frantic
to meet her surely they might have shown a little more
enthusiasm? Their names were Rose and Marni, and
they were, at a guess, fifteen. "Not sisters, cousins," they
insisted when Kate was introduced. Rose had long fair
hair like frozen honey, Marni's hair was black, frizzing
along the edges, although she'd obviously plastered it
stiff with lacquer. Richard, the bad-tempered boy, still
looking bad-tempered, was seated opposite with his parents on either side of him. They were introduced as Mr.
and Mrs. Blunt. At the other end of the table sat Mr.
and Mrs. Tweedle, small, grey-haired, and smiling
through their spectacles, like a couple of elderly teddy
bears. The Mad Hatter sat on Mrs. Blunt's left. Kate
didn't catch his name but identified him by the tadpoles
on his tie. He was long and thin and not much chin or
hair.

Miss Dilys Darlington was the last to arrive. "So very
sorry one and all, please be kind and forgive," she said,
twirling her string of beads, "but something came to me

while I was out along the beach this afternoon. So very significant — I just had to go and write it down."

"A world in a grain of sand?" the Mad Hatter inquired, and Miss Darlington accelerated the necklace so that it made a transparent wheel and smiled, "How well you understand!"

"And this is my niece Kate," said Aunt Poppy. Miss Darlington abandoned the beads in mid-air and pressed Kate's hand. "Ah, but Kate and I have met already, haven't we, Kate?" she purred as if they'd recently been fellow conspirators on the Orient Express, passing a secret code to each other hidden inside a ham sandwich, instead of colliding outside the bathroom door.

Mad, all mad, Kate decided, bats, loony, loopy, crazy clucks every one of them. She was glad to see that her portion of fried fish looked normal.

Aunt Poppy offered Mrs. Blunt the bottle of ketchup.

"No, thank you."

"Vinegar, then?"

Mrs. Blunt looked at the vinegar sideways down her nose for a fraction of a second and said "Thank you, no. Sauce Tartare is the only garnish I care for with fried fish." Aunt Poppy's smile changed to a look of faded apology. "The chef at the Splendide serves an excellent Sauce Tartare," Mrs. Blunt continued, attacking her naked fish with small, angry bites. "They keep a very good table at the Splendide."

"A lot of messed-up fancy French food if you ask me, no nourishment in it," Mr. Blunt barked. "That's right, isn't it, Richard?"

"You needn't ask Richard. He never missed a course last August, did you, Richard?" Mrs. Blunt asked, but Richard had filled his mouth · with buttered roll and stayed neutral.

From the other end of the table Mrs. Tweedle's spectacles lit up like kindly head-lamps. "We always look forward to the fish at Sea View, Miss Lucas. So very delicious. William says your fish never gives him the slightest trouble, don't you, William?"

"That's what I always say," Mr. Tweedle agreed, and smiled a warm secret smile at his wife as though they were holding hands below the table.

"I like your dress, it's smashing," Marni said to Kate. Rose gave the gold mini-dress a glance and said over Kate's head, "Madge Turner at school had one the very same, don't you remember, Marni? Terrible she looked in it."

Edna the maid came round with second helpings of chips. "Please please, no more for me," Miss Darlington implored. "Remember, I'm trying to shed a little."

The Mad Hatter, munching, muttered about, "This too, too solid flesh," and Miss Darlington changed her mind. "Well, perhaps just three more, Edna," she said, and forgot to look at her plate until Edna had loaded a whole steaming haystack on to it.

"Edna! Have pity!" Miss Darlington moaned when she allowed herself to notice her plate again, and Richard opened his mouth to say well, she needn't eat them all, need she, and Miss Darlington said no, of course she needn't, and laughed crossly.

"That's Tendresse des Arbres you've got on, isn't it?" Rose asked. Kate said it was and Marni said it looked terrific, really it did, and Kate asked how did Rose know. "Oh, everyone's wearing it, you see it all over the place," Rose said. "Don't you find it goes sticky?" Then Aunt Poppy and the maid cleared away the plates and brought in the sweet. It was Peach Surprise, Aunt Poppy announced. No one was really astonished.

"The chef at the Splendide did a most excellent peaches and brandy," Mrs. Blunt commented, poking with her spoon. "Real peaches, of course." She poked so hard that some of the jelly, which was tough and elastic, bounced out of her plate and landed on the cloth opposite the Mad Hatter. He scraped it up and ate it. "All contributions gladly received and promptly acknowledged," he said, and Mrs. Blunt looked offended while everybody else laughed.

"Can I tempt you to just a hint more cream, Miss Darlington?" Aunt Poppy stood with the jug poised. Aunt Dilly eyed it as if it were a phial of poison and said, "Not for me, no really, dear Miss Lucas," and then looked with eyes of envy at the thick pale flood falling into the plate of the Mad Hatter.

"You'll excuse William, won't you?" Mrs. Tweedle asked the guests in general. "But the doctor says it is so very important for him to swallow his medicine just before the digestive juices take over." She passed a little glass filled with white cloudy liquid to Mr. Tweedle and he said, "Thank you, my dear," and raised the glass and drank a toast, looking at Mrs. Tweedle as if his digestive juices were singing the Hallelujah Chorus especially for her.

Kate pursued the last crescent of fruit round and round her plate. It was as slippery and evasive as a goldfish. Three meals a day, she counted, breakfast, lunch and tea, and twenty-one days to go. That made sixty-three meals. All as odd as this one.

Aunt Poppy was inviting Miss Darlington to take another wafer biscuit. Only vanity she said, nothing to them, and Miss Darlington said she never could resist a wafer biscuit and didn't try.

"No. No cheese, thank you," Mrs. Blunt said without even looking.

"Richard likes cheese, don't you, Richard?" Mr. Blunt asked.

Miss Darlington murmured, "Well perhaps just a morsel. So full of protein."

"The doctor said most emphatically not, thank you very much, dear Miss Lucas," Mrs. Tweedle smiled. "Isn't that what the doctor said, William?" And Mr. Tweedle explained to the Mad Hatter why the doctor had been so emphatic about no cheese.

"The cheeses in Yugoslavia —" Mrs. Blunt began, but no one was listening. "Good old British mousetrap, eh, Richard?" Mr. Blunt declared, and dug in his knife deeply.

Rose asked how many kinds of eye-shadow Kate had, and Kate told her she had four. Rose had nine, she thought the silvery ones were rather fun. Kate said she hadn't tried the silvery ones yet, and Rose said actually they were rather dreamy though it wasn't everybody who could wear them, you had to be the type.

"No," pronounced Miss Darlington, sighing, "definitely not another crumb," and the meal was over.

"Come up to our room and talk, why don't you?" Marni invited as the girls scraped back their chairs. Rose frowned but Kate pretended she hadn't noticed and said all right, she would. "For these and all Thy mercies," said Mr. and Mrs. Tweedle, standing with their eyes closed and their elderly hands folded like good children, while other people noticed just in time and froze until it was over, and the Mad Hatter said "Amen!" in a loud jolly voice.

Rose and Marni led the way upstairs to the big room at the front of the house. "This is ours." As soon as the door was closed they flopped on to the big bed which was so wide that they could all three lie across it without touching. Now they could laugh. They all needed to. It was like being let out of prison, or like elastic when it snaps. "Oh gosh, wasn't it funny?" They lay there bouncing gently and giggling. Rose's honey-coloured hair poured down to touch the floor. Marni had rolled over on her face and was holding her stomach; she had hiccups. "It's my gastric juices, they're all confused," she explained, jerking painfully and fighting her persistent laughter.

Rose sat up and commanded, "Don't! I've laughed long enough," and was at once seized with another gale of mirth.

'It was when the Mad Hatter scooped the jelly off the ₁oth and ate it," Kate gasped. "I nearly died!"

Marni hooted like a laying hen and swivelled round. *"Who* did you say?"

"The Mad Hatter."

"Rose, did you hear what she said — the Mad Hatter?"

"I heard!"

The bed rocked as they shared this new joke.

"What is his real name?"

"Mr. J. L. S. Smith — that's what it says on his letters. When he gets any letters."

"It's our poor Aunt Dilly who gets the letters. It's her poems, they come back to her nearly every breakfast, in long pale envelopes."

"The Mad Hatter is much better than Mr. Smith!"

"Much, much better."

"He's a bit of a mystery, anyway. Every afternoon and every evening he goes off, riding on your aunt's bicycle."

"Where does he go?"

"We haven't found out yet."

"Have you got names for them all?" Marni asked, "go on — tell!"

Kate's tongue was inspired. "Only for the Tweedles."

"The Tweedles? What do you call them?"

"I should have thought it was obvious. Tweedle Him and Tweedle Her!"

They lay back snorting and crowing. "My hair," Rose complained. "It's getting all messed up."

"Oh, bother your hair," said Marni comfortably.

24

Gradually her hiccups and their hilarity subsided. Little ripples of amusement still shook them from time to time, but they were too lazy to pursue them and too well satisfied, too full of content and fried fish and Peach Surprise.

Kate, staring at the cracks in the ceiling, hoped this would go on for a long time. She felt eased and happy, good and thankful, like she did sometimes when she'd just been to church or got a top mark for her essay. The sensation of walking on tiptoe all the time had gone. Her face, which had grown stiff because it knew it was being looked at by strangers, forgot now that it was visible. Talking wasn't difficult any more, you didn't need to translate what you thought into language, you just opened your mouth. All the bogey-men had gone home, there could be nothing inside her wardrobe except the things she had put there. Even the bathroom manœuvre would be easy, she would rattle the door or shout "Righty-ho, then!" if she felt like it. She would go downstairs by way of the banisters, they were longer and steeper than the ones at home. With Marni and Rose she would natter her way through three weeks of meals, and lie stretched out on their bed, or on the sandhills, and they would tell each other things and feel comfortable and happy and wise.

Rose slid off the bed and went across to the mirror. "My hair! I told you it was getting messed up!" She began to brush it smooth again with long clever strokes of the brush, watching her reflection all the time.

Marni wiggled her toes derisively. "You and your hair!"

"Yours is a sight."

"Well, who cares!"

The clock interrupted them by striking eight. "I didn't know it was as late as that!" Marni heaved herself up and went to join Rose. Now both hairbrushes were going, stroke for stroke.

"What shoes are you going to wear?"

"These."

"Your feet'll be killed."

"I don't care. Anyway, they won't."

Kate didn't stir. She was inventing ways to get from one corner of the ceiling to the other by the cracks, pretending it was a map. In her bedroom at home she knew all the quickest ways.

"You're not going to wear those earrings, are you?"

"What's wrong with them?"

"You might lose them, that's all."

Rose said, "I won't lose them."

"You'd never find them again, not if we walk along the sandhills." The hairbrushes were working steadily, keeping time.

"When do they turn on the fairy lights along the Esplanade?" Kate asked. "I'm dying to see them."

One of the brushes faltered, the pace had become uneven.

"I'd like to see it when the lights go on," Kate added. "That's if we could."

The brushes slowed. Now they had stopped.

"The best place for you to go," Rose said carefully, "would be along past the bandstand, above the bathing pool. You'd get a super view from there."

The hairbrushes went into operation again, each stroke light and very precise. Kate lay still. She'd got the message. She felt cheated and miserable, flat as a cold pancake. All the warmth was sucked out of her.

"It's super down by the bathing-pool," Marni said. "Can you swim?"

"Yes." She wished she'd had the courage to say didn't they know she was still a little girl and only allowed to paddle at the shallow end. I'm just a kid. I have to go to bed at half-past eight and remember to clean my teeth.

"We're going to be late," Marni fussed, and Rose said yes, she knew, so what, and went on brushing.

Marni stuck her head out of the window and squealed, "There they are!" And Rose told her to be her age and said, "Peter's the fair one. The other's Mike."

"You said he was tall." Marni was behind the curtain, squinting.

"He is tall."

"Not as tall as Edgar."

"I never said he was as tall as Edgar."

"We'd better go, hadn't we?"

"No hurry. I'm not ready yet."

Kate listened to Marni fidgeting while Rose took her time. At last Rose said, "All right, come on if you're coming." She slung her jersey over her shoulder and crossed to the door. Kate raised herself on her elbow to watch her. There couldn't be any other or better name for her than Rose. Just to look at her made you ache with envy and a kind of joy. There used to be a girl at school who was like that. And there was a picture hanging on the wall of the art room — a queen or a princess, a long, long time ago. Somebody who was dead now.

Rose paused as she came past the bed and said, "We could go and look at the shops after breakfast tomorrow if you like. And I could set your hair for you. I bet I could make it look terrific."

"Oh, come *on*," Marni urged. "And there's nothing wrong with Kate's hair."

"Well — be seeing you then." Rose and Marni made their exit, leaving solid trails of perfume behind them. Now they were on their way downstairs.

Clever, aren't you, Kate said to herself and to a couple of flies on the wall. You ought to have seen it coming, it was sticking out a mile. Well, let them go. She heaved herself off the bed and went over to the window and looked down into the street. Rose and the tall boy with the smarmed fair hair were walking in front, hands linked. That must be Peter. He was talking. Marni and the boy with red hair followed. Instead of holding hands they were walking a foot or two apart, looking at each other sideways. Marni had to gallop a bit to keep up. It didn't look comfortable. You could tell they didn't know what to say to each other.

When they were out of sight Kate studied her own reflection fiercely across the wreck of the dressing-table. Nobody was going to set her hair for her tomorrow, that was one sure thing. And that bit about going to **look at** the shops — Rose hadn't said it to be kind, she'd said it because she wanted to be liked. If you looked as gorgeous as Rose you probably needed to be sure you were liked.

Kate went to her room and pulled on a cardigan. When she came downstairs the Tweedles were in the hall. They had just come in, and Mrs. Tweedle was unwinding a scarf from Mr. Tweedle's neck. "Just in time for his favourite programme," she smiled at Kate. "Going out, are you, dear? Will you be warm enough?" The sound of the telly oozed through from the lounge.

Once outside, Kate felt better. She didn't hurry — she didn't want to catch up with the others. It was pleasant to be by herself. Who wanted to giggle and natter? The pavement in the main street was crowded but she dodged her way through, the excitement of being alone gave spring to her step. Already above the smells from the cafés and fish bars and sweet shops she could smell the sharp smell of the sea.

Now she had reached the Esplanade. It was, as Aunt Poppy's postcards had promised it would be, edged with white marble balustrades. There were palms growing in urns and brilliant beds of flowers set out in patterns, not one leaf or petal out of place. Flights of white steps like the stairs in the last act of a pantomime curved from the pavement down to the beach. There it was — Sunny Bay!

The bay was certainly sunny. It was also crumpled, trodden, flattened, scooped, bashed, slashed across with bicycle tracks and the tracks of prams, scattered with toffee papers and ice-cream cartons and the tired ruins of

c

one day's castles, moats, gateways and walls. It was studded with deck-chair marks and the excavations of dogs. The remains of one day's holiday stretched a long way out. The sand, like soft brown sugar that has been hammered and scored, scuffed, heaped, used and abused, extended right to the edge of a flat and unresponsive sea.

The beach was deserted now except for an exploring dog and an empty paper-bag that had caught the breeze and hadn't decided which direction it was heading for. It travelled scrapily over the sand. All the holiday-makers had crowded into their cars and buses, their hotels and guest houses, coffee bars, dance halls and cinemas, leaving the night's tide to clear up the day's mess.

None of the curving marble flights of steps tempted Kate. She ran past them all quickly, swallowing her disappointment. Was there something wrong with the seaside or something wrong with her? A few years ago a couple of yards of second-hand sand would have been all she wanted: enough to bury her legs in long humps like railway tunnels and then watch the cracks coming when she wiggled her ankles; enough to dig a hole as deep as her extended arm could scratch and see the sides of it collapsing into the little centre of dampness which grew bigger and darker and colder, the more furiously she scooped.

Kate's indignation had carried her farther and faster than she realized. She passed the last flight of steps, the last chewing-gum machine, the last palm in its urn, the last geometrical flower-bed. Iron railings now took the place of the white marble. The road rose a little as it reached the end of the bay and turned inward, the land to seaward swept out in a long tongue of uneven rock. She looked back across the curve of the bay. There was the blind house, right opposite. What a view there must be from the front windows! It was too far for her to see whether they too were curtained.

She ducked below the railings and set off across the rocks. Of course she should have put on her jeans and gym shoes; already she could feel the rough shell-encrusted surface through the thin soles of her gold sandals. People didn't go climbing rocks in gold minidresses. The posh models did, the ones in the glossy magazines. All right, that was what she could be. She found a platform of seaweed that crackled when she put her weight on it but seemed steady enough. Now she posed, arms on hips and her tummy stuck out, the way the models did. She pulled some of her hair round, inviting the wind to spread it about for her so that it would look right for the photograph, but the wind wasn't playing. Her feet sank through the seaweed to the slimy mass below, and she narrowly escaped falling.

Her ankles were damp — suddenly the trodden seaweed smelled outrageously exciting. Who wanted to fool around pretending to be a model? The stillness of rock pools was broken by the tracks of creatures too small to be seen, going about their business. She explored one pool after another, splashily. A scavenging seagull rose in front of her, yellow-footed and fierce.

All the time the sound of the sea was coming nearer, not the noise of waves collapsing on the flat sand, but of waves that broke against rocks. She had walked a long way now. The noise of the waves had swallowed all the noises from the town behind her. The air here felt colder, fresh and lonely. She passed the point of the promontory. The rocks here fell jaggedly away towards the sea.

She had come now to a little cove and was looking down on a steep, white-pebbled beach no broader or longer than a drawing-room. Waves that had already broken ran up it in long foamy tongues, washing all the crevices, filling pools and emptying them, sucking at the pebbles before they dropped them and slid back again to the open sea. The pebbles rattled and fell, waiting for the next wave to disturb them. Pieces of creamy froth were caught in the seaweed and stayed there, tugging to get away.

She saw the boy before he saw her. He was standing like a statue, with his toes curved around a ledge of rock that stuck out where the water was deep and unbroken before it came running up into the cove. He wore bathing trunks and was standing very straight. He looked skinny, taller than he did when she'd seen him on the landing of Aunt Poppy's house. Although he was some distance off she could hear him breathing in an odd harsh kind of way, as if each breath hurt. She thought he was talking to himself — no, he was counting.

"One — two — three — four —" He drew himself up even taller, then sagged suddenly and crouched down, pushing an arm across his face. After a moment he straightened and took up his stance again. She could see that his face was dull and white, his eyes very wide open. He fidgeted about with his feet, testing his balance, altering the position of his toes, then altering them again, lifting his heels an inch and dropping them.

He raised his head higher. "This time," she heard him say, "this time, I swear it." He began to count again, more slowly. Kate ached, watching him; the insides of her hands felt sticky. He had counted as far as six when suddenly, with a little cry and a jerk he pushed himself into a dive and fell forwards into the water.

It wasn't a good dive by any standards. Head too high, too much splash, hands spread and finger-tips searching for the water before they had reached it. But when his shoulders appeared above the water again Kate found that she was clapping.

A few strokes brought him to the shelf of rock. He pulled himself out, then heard her applause and turned his head sharply.

"Oh, it's you. What do you think you're doing? Still snooping?"

She said, "I was watching. I didn't think you'd do it."

"Why shouldn't I do it?"

"It was high. I don't like going off anything as high as that."

He shook water out of his hair and eyes and spat and said, "It was easy. You saw."

"All right, so I did see."

"I'll do it again."

She was about to protest, but he climbed up to his perch and this time without any hesitation repeated the dive. When he came out of the water again he was shaking all over and his skin was blotchy. He reached for a towel and scrubbed at his head, then shuffled his way stickily into an old mac. All the time he was whistling in jerks between his chattering teeth.

Kate said, "I thought you and your dad were going for a climb on the cliffs."

"My mum had a headache, so he stayed with her."

"Does she often have headaches?"

"Everybody has headaches sometimes."

"Why didn't you go to the pictures, then?"

"So you were snooping," he said, "out there on the landing. I knew you were."

"Anyway, why don't you go to the swimming-pool?"

"I come here to practise. Too many people at the pool. It spoils your concentration."

"Concentration my foot," she said rudely. "You were practising being frightened."

"Shut up, why don't you?" he said. "Fat lot you know about it."

"I do know. I'm always scared of the diving-board."

"You wait till you see my father, he goes off the highest board of all. I'm going to the swimming-pool with him in the morning."

Kate recognized the challenge and said, "My father's dead, ages ago."

Richard didn't say anything. People didn't when you

told them your father was dead. They dried up as if it had been unfair of you to mention it.

"Do you like it here?" he asked after three waves had come and gone while she counted them.

"Do you?"

"It's all right. We come here every year. Usually we stay at the Splendide, but this year we were late booking and we couldn't get in."

"I expect you think Sea View's pretty crummy," she suggested, feeling a traitor.

"I didn't say so."

"Your mum did." She counted four more waves. Then she said "Miss Lucas is my aunt."

He said "So what?" but she knew that somehow the score between them had evened up.

Richard stuffed the towel into the pocket of his mac. It was too big and hung out. "Come on, then, if you're coming," he said. He led the way back across the rocks with Kate a few yards behind, slipping and sliding in an effort to keep up. She felt the strap of one sandal break, then the other heel was wrenched, the sole cracked. The air was growing dark; it was more difficult to see the rocks, though the pools had brightened, catching colour from the sky.

Just as they came to the start of the Esplanade the lights went on, one after another, right round the bay from end to end, as neat and smooth as a giant zipper.

"Gosh!" Kate said when she had got back her breath, "is it always like that?"

"Unless the match blows out," Richard said in a rude, happy kind of way. "Let's go back along the edge of the water. We've just about got time."

"What do you mean — time?"

"You have to watch it, crossing the bay when the tide's coming in. It comes in very fast."

"Not as fast as all that," she objected. The waves still had a long way to come, though already they had covered some of the untidy beach and swallowed up the rubbish.

"I'm only telling you," he said, "and there are notices. It does come in fast."

"All right, I heard."

Down at its edge the water looked heavy and thick. Kate found she was limping, she took off the sandals so that the cool wash of the sea reached her bare feet. The water stung, and thin threads of seaweed grabbed at her and wrapped themselves round her ankles. She stood still, burrowing with her toes into the wet, moving mass of the sand.

"I could stay here for hours."

"You couldn't. I told you. And you've gone and dropped your sandals."

"I don't care." She fished for the floating sandals and threw first one of them and then the other as far as she could out into the water. It seemed a reasonable and pleasant thing to do. She couldn't see them any more but she enjoyed thinking about them, a pair of Golden Vanities, dipping and bobbing about in the waves, until finally they sank, to make homes for crabs.

Richard said, "You are a loon, Kate. What did you want to do that for? Anyway, come on!"

She was enjoying herself, each wave crept further up her legs; their pull had become stronger. "You do go on, Richard," she complained. "We've got loads of time."

"We haven't. I told you it was dangerous. People have been drowned."

"Drowned?" He was trying to scare her of course, because she'd watched him when he was scared. But already she could see that as each wave raised itself it seemed as if the whole mass of water might tilt and slide right across the sand. The waves had become savage, violent, not the tame wrinkles of water that she had watched earlier.

"Better run for it," Richard advised. Now they were both running, prancing, laughing, stamping ankle-high in the water; dryness and wetness became one and the same thing as they made their way back along the beach.

~⊰ 3 ⊱~

THE STRING of lights spread like a necklace along the curve of the Esplanade. The marble steps and terraces were crowded. People were walking more slowly now — the light shone on their hair, their mouths and eyes were very dark, their faces had become more important. They were like people out of a play. As Kate and Richard climbed up one of the flights of steps, they passed Rose and Marni with Peter and the boy with red hair. Rose was leaning against the marble balustrade looking beautiful. She belonged to the play and knew her part in it. Peter was still talking. Marni and the boy with red hair were pulling leaves off the bushes and dropping them in very small pieces, not saying anything. The red-haired boy stared at Rose over Marni's head.

"I say, did you see? Those are the girls from Sea View — and how!" Kate said, when they'd gone past. She expected Richard would want to laugh, would say something funny about Rose and Marni all glammed up like a couple of Beauty Queens, but he only asked, "So what?" and looked at Kate as if she was being dim or had spoken the wrong lines.

She said "The tall boy's Peter."

"I know. They're staying at the Splendide. They

stayed there last year," Richard said. Then he slowed and stopped. "My towel, I had it in my pocket. It must have dropped out. I'll nip back and look for it."

"Will I come with you?"

"Don't be daft," he said. "What would be the sense of both of us going?" and disappeared in the crowds.

Kate felt lonely and cross again. "Well, here I am," she announced as she reached Sea View and saw the sauce bottles between the lace curtains. The house didn't seem to recognize her. She had hoped that with any luck it might feel a little like coming home, but it didn't. At the end of three weeks, she thought, I'll go bouncing up those steps as if I'd been born there, knowing how the stairs and the door-handles feel without looking — but she didn't really believe it now. The evening was growing dark; she would have to go in.

The telly was still bleating through the door of the lounge. Mr. and Mrs. Tweedle were setting off for bed, working their way stair by stair, Mr. Tweedle in front holding on to the banister rail and sliding his hand up it, inch after inch. Mrs. Tweedle came close behind him, a little breathless, laden with rugs, books, newspapers, a vacuum flask, a pillow and a plump hot-water bottle in a pink velvet cover.

One of the papers dropped and Kate ran up and picked it up and tucked it under Mrs. Tweedle's elbow. "Thank you, my dear, so very kind," Mrs. Tweedle said. Then she exclaimed, "Oh, how stupid of me, this is William's dining-room bottle of pills. Whatever am I bringing it upstairs with me for? Just take it from me, dear, will you, and set it on the sideboard. So much to remember, no wonder my poor head gets in a muddle." Kate took the little bottle and slid it into the pocket of her cardigan. "Now then, William, up the wooden hill to the Land of Nod," Mrs. Tweedle urged, and the procession began to move again.

Kate stood in the hall, waiting. Even when the stairs at last were clear she didn't stir. This was going to be the hardest part of all. She could go and goggle with the rest of them in the lounge, she supposed, but she didn't want to. But it wasn't possible for her to climb those stairs and go into that room and close the door and be alone until morning unless she had some kind of a blessing. A day couldn't end just like that, there had to be a pattern for finishing it. There was always a pattern at home. She must find Aunt Poppy and say goodnight; it would only be polite to do that and it would provide a pattern. It would draw a line across the page. But there was no sign of Aunt Poppy, and the closed doors in the hall gave no clue where to start looking for her. Why not whoop the way she always whooped when she came in from school? "Hallo-o-o!" But all the awkwardness of being new in this house froze up her tongue.

The front door opened and Miss Darlington was wafted in, festooned in scarves, with dozens of loose ends, like the little cherubs you sometimes see on painted ceilings. She clutched at Kate.

"My dear! Did you see it?"

A sea serpent? A tidal wave? Or perhaps just a couple of fire engines? "See what, Aunt Dilly?"

"Don't tell me you missed it! In the sky!"

Kate said: "I think I must have," wondering whether a flypast of angels had gone over while she'd been throwing her golden sandals out to sea.

"It was fabulous, there aren't words — there just are no words for a sunset like that. I stood there aching for words — aching!" Miss Darlington's scarves became entangled with her necklace and with the paper packet she was clutching. She breathed chocolate biscuits and delight and lavender water.

"The daily miracle," she declared, straightening herself out. "To think it happens every day. Music might do it honour, but I defy you to find *words*. Here — have one!" She pushed the packet of chocolate biscuits at Kate, who helped herself; then she turned for the stairs. "All that magnificent sky-streaked ferocity!" she sighed, "and every evening since the Creation!"

Before Miss Darlington disappeared Kate remembered to ask where she would find her aunt.

"The door at the end of the passage leading to the kitchen," Miss Darlington directed with her mouth full, and ascended.

When she had gone Kate turned for the door at the end of the passage, then paused, trying to decide whether she should knock. In a hotel — even in a guest house — you probably knocked. Did you knock when it was your aunt's room and you had come to say goodnight? There ought to be a book of rules. She could hear voices coming from inside the room, a man's voice and the voice of her aunt. They were talking more loudly than people usually talk, not always waiting for each other to finish. Could it be an argument? Kate had decided that she would skip saying goodnight after all, when the door opened and the Mad Hatter came out.

She was glad it was him. She felt warm and comfortable, waiting for him to say something funny or friendly or uncle-ish. Come on, any little joke — even if it was silly she was ready and willing to laugh. But he didn't seem to notice her. He went straight through the hall and into the lounge, closing the door behind him.

She knocked without giving herself time to think about it and her aunt's voice instructed her to come in.

"It's me, Kate."

"Why, Kate! I wondered where you'd got to, child. Is there anything you want?"

"I just came to say goodnight."

"Yes, of course."

Well you've said it now, haven't you, what else are you waiting for? Her aunt was sitting at a desk crammed with untidy papers. There was a crumpled handkerchief lying among them. Her face was tired and patchy, her hair frizzy and in wisps, and she was wearing bedroom slippers. Kate bade farewell forever to the suave and elegant relative whom she had cherished in her imagination ever since she'd heard of this holiday.

Aunt Poppy blew her nose and stuck pins back into her hair. "Well, have you been out to see the sights? What do you think of Sunny Bay?"

Kate said: "It's very nice, thank you," and wished it need not sound so lame.

"The place has changed a lot since your father's day. He would hardly know it now," Aunt Poppy said unexpectedly.

"Did he live here?" She felt stupid that she needed to ask.

"Didn't he ever tell you?"

"He told me it was somewhere in the country."

It was curious to be talking about her father. So little remained of him now, and they were the old unforgettable things, always the same things. Sometimes she went over and over what she remembered in the hope of discovering something new. Her father — of course she would know about her own father! But trying to remember wasn't any use, nothing extra was ever discovered. It was like staring at a picture that you knew by heart to find out something that you hadn't noticed before. But you didn't find it.

"Our home was near here when we were children," Aunt Poppy said. "Our father had a farm a couple of miles inland." Aunt Poppy had a different picture of her father to remember.

"He never said it was a farm." Imagining grown-ups when they were children was tricky — sometimes it turned out to be funny; mostly you couldn't believe it anyway. Perhaps it was better just to stick to the old picture.

"Farming wasn't in your father's line — too clever at his books," Aunt Poppy said.

"I suppose that was why he never brought us here on a visit."

43

Aunt Poppy pushed at the papers and laughed and said, "Your mother wouldn't care much for the country, would she?" This was right enough, but not Aunt Poppy's business. Mum was too little, her heels were too high, she didn't like cows, the rain did things to her hair. You should have seen her hair and her heels yesterday!

"We could go and look at the farm if you like," Aunt Poppy volunteered. "If I can get away for an hour or so."

"Oh, all right." She made it sound off-hand on purpose, pretending it didn't matter to her whether they looked at it or not.

There remained the awkward ritual of goodnight. "You'd better run off now," Aunt Poppy said, as if this was bothering her too. "I expect you're tired."

Without really meaning to, Kate said, "It's you that's tired." Aunt Poppy didn't answer, so Kate went on: "Mrs. Blunt didn't mean to be so horrid at tea, Aunt Poppy. It was because she had a headache."

Her aunt's face flared redder and the colour spread like a stain down her neck. "If they didn't want to come here they should have stayed away. I'm sure I always do my best."

"I told you. She had a headache. Richard said so."

"Yes. Hadn't you better go to bed now, child?"

The floor between them seemed to stretch out a very long way. Kate moved towards the door. "Goodnight, Aunt Poppy."

"Goodnight and sleep well. And Kate —"

"Yes?"

"That letter — did you write it?"

"Not yet. But I'm going to."

"Write it tonight; then you can post it first thing in the morning."

"Yes, Aunt Poppy."

"Don't forget, child."

So now she was out in the hall again and the stairs were lying in wait for her. As she went up them she felt that a drawbridge was being raised behind her and wouldn't be let down again until the morning. She stuck out her tongue at the clock because it began to strike when she wasn't ready for it. Its voice was still surprising, like someone talking in a foreign language. Once inside her door she had to feel around on the wall for the light switch. The lampshade had water lilies on it — she hadn't noticed that before; they only showed up when the light was lit.

The mirror in the wardrobe reflected an untidy ruffled person in a gold mini-dress which had concertina'd up her stomach in creases; her hair hung any old way, her face was shiny — it tasted of salt when she licked. Her legs and feet were bare and streaked with sand. If Aunt Poppy hadn't been so tired and upset surely she would have said something. This wasn't what Kate had intended to look like at the end of the first evening of her holiday. She had planned a long, thoughtful session with her diary before she went to bed, something she could show Hazel — what there had been to eat and the view from her room and what other people wore and who she thought she was going to choose

D

for friends. She would read it out to Hazel in install-
ments in the bicycle shed. "Well sometimes you *feel* like
that about a person straightaway — you just *know!*"
Hazel, released from the caravan and sardines would nod
enviously and say, "Oh, yes! Of course!"

But things had turned out so different, so awkward
and unlikely, that she decided she would skip the diary
altogether. A verbal report on Sunny Bay would allow
her to pick out the best bits and would be less binding.

The music from the Splendide was coming in through
the window, loud, sweet and clear. Kate pushed back the
curtains and craned her neck to get a better view. People
were moving in and out of the strips of light that spread
through the windows across the hotel lawn. You could
see the boys' shiny hair and the pale stockings of the
girls. Somewhere in the dark pit of the yard below her
window a cat inspected a dustbin.

It was all too much to bear. The room felt like a
prison. She couldn't stay here all night through until the
morning. All right, if the room was a prison she would
demonstrate that she could escape from it. She'd
planned an escape route by daylight; she could remember it now. There was nothing to stop her. Guests were
Requested to be Punctual for Meals and Kindly to
Leave the Bathroom as they would Wish to Find it, and
not to Drip Dry Articles of Clothing in the Bedrooms,
but there was no rule to say they weren't allowed to
climb out of their windows if they felt like it, was there?
Of course it was going to look pretty silly if anyone saw,
but that was a risk she was prepared to take. The flavour

of danger pleased her; a taste of rebellion was just what she needed.

She pulled on a pair of jeans, tucking in the ends of the mini-dress as casually as if it had been a shirt-tail. This was one episode she would skip telling Hazel, but she intended to enjoy it.

She was out across the window-sill, and by way of a drain-pipe soon made the awkward descent to the low, flat-angled roof of the kitchen. Under her bare feet the tiles still felt warm after the day's sun. She scrambled side-ways along them, arms and legs spread out like a fly on a tilted wall, then stared into the blackness of the yard below her where dish-cloths swam like pieces of skin off hot milk. They appeared and disappeared lazily on their invisible clothes-line. She lay on her stomach inelegantly and lowered herself, allowing her feet to drop over the edge of the roof, then pawed about until her toe found the solid lid of a dustbin. With a yank, a twist and a leap she landed on the concrete surface of the yard.

The bin lid, rocking, sent out a cymbal crash. Kate crouched low, waiting for the thin golden rectangle around the back door to widen and thrust an accusing light right across the yard, but the shape of the rectangle did not alter. So! There she was. No one had heard. Her own cleverness pleased her; she came out from behind the bins and performed a little dance of triumph, slap-ping the soles of her feet down with delicate precision, no heavier than leaves when they fall.

Her heel landed on the hard edge of a saucer. There was a rattle, and she felt the wetness of the cat's neglected supper and stopped fooling. Careful, Kate, you've been lucky so far. She could smell the sour smell of the bushes at the bottom of the yard and decided to go on and make a complete survey of Sea View's territory. There wasn't much to see or much sense in what she was doing; it was a child's game—but she was in the mood to act like a child.

The ground beneath the bushes was unexpectedly soggy and sometimes the branches got into her eyes and tangled her hair. Now she was through them, had reached the wall that divided Aunt Poppy's back-yard from the garden of the blind house. It was a high wall, but there were enough jutting-out pieces to tempt her to climb it. Up she went. She could have scaled a castle wall tonight, with a black moat lying sulkily below her, and ranks of bow-men on the battlements with their bows strung. The top of the wall was smothered deep in ivy.

As she reached the top she reached the moonlight. If Miss Darlington had waited for this moon she would have demanded a whole symphony to celebrate it. It was large and white; it looked faintly rough, like eggshell. It was not quite round — so that you knew it was real and not a picture. You could feel it; it was nearly warm. Minute by minute it was lifting itself over the roof of the blind house. With fingers and toes anchored deep in the stems of the ivy, Kate watched it.

The back door of Aunt Poppy's house had opened. A latch clicked. Kate turned in time to see a wing of light fall across the bins. Then the door closed. She heard footsteps. They were coming nearer; the white bunting of tea towels stirred as someone passed through them.

She ducked her head and crouched as low as she could into the bitter-smelling ivy; then she froze. Now she could hear the bushes shaking. Now someone had stepped out from them, and was close to her.

It was someone she recognized, the Mad Hatter alias Mr. J. L. S. Smith. He straightened as he emerged from the branches, then took a couple of steps nearer the wall. He's seen me, Kate thought, and waited for him to tell her to come down. Lucky it was him, perhaps between them they might turn this into a joke, a moonlit "I Spy". But he didn't speak. He hadn't seen her. He was looking past her, looking over the wall to the upper windows of the blind house. The moonlight showed her his face clearly. There was an expression on it that reminded her — yes, reminded her of Richard's face as she had seen it earlier this evening when he stood at the water's edge persuading himself that he could dive. It was a look of preparation for something he must do and couldn't. Still he didn't move. All Kate's will-power was now bent on preventing herself from sneezing; the reek of the ivy stems had gone up her nose. One of the leaves prickled the soft place at the back of her neck. She wanted badly to scratch.

The music from the Splendide had snapped off. It was now so quiet that she could hear the Mad Hatter breathing, and a long way off the sound of the breathing sea. Go on, she urged him silently, whatever it is go on and do it, why don't you? It can't be so terrible. But he was still there, and little by little she saw the sternness fade from his face. His face looked silly, the way no grown-up person's face ought to look. Whatever it was, he'd found himself a reason to excuse himself from doing it. After a moment he turned and went back the way he had come, and soon the kitchen door opened and closed again.

Kate sneezed and scratched and blew out long breaths of relief. Other people and the things they did and the way they did them were peculiar, but they'd probably think it was peculiar of her to be nesting in the ivy at this hour of the night, and she was glad she didn't have to do any explaining. But she couldn't sit out here for ever; it was time she was getting back.

She didn't discover how stiff she was until she tried to straighten up. She wobbled and almost lost her balance; for a moment of panic she thought she was going to fall down on the wrong side of the wall. Her cardigan had caught in the ivy — she had to wriggle one of the sleeves off and yank before it came clear. Sliding down off the wall was a clumsy business; this time if there had been any bow-men on the look-out for invaders their arrows would have made a hedgehog of her within seconds. Now she was through the bushes and spread out again on the kitchen roof above the moving maze of dish-cloths. A transistor was going full blast below her; she could feel the beat of it in her finger-tips as she worked her way along, crabwise.

The drain-pipe seemed to have stretched out an extra yard or two since she'd come down it, but she didn't allow herself time to think. Somebody's bath-water gurgled warmly down it. Now she was hoisting herself over the window-sill, and at last was back inside her own room.

She remembered the letter she had to write, and the success of her expedition made her decide to write it. She found the writing-paper and envelopes tucked into the pocket at the back of her suitcase. Mum had put the right stamps on the envelopes, but she had also done something else — she had written the name and address.

She didn't have to do that for me, Kate thought. I could have written the envelopes; there was no need for her. Mum's writing was large and loopy and untidy, all the things that Mum wasn't. "Mr. and Mrs. Godfrey Pennington" — and then the address in Paris.

It was very difficult to write the letter. "The train was hot — I read my book — it stopped for a long time at one of the stations (cross out 'it' and write in 'the train') — Aunt Poppy is very nice — Sunny Bay is nice — I hope you are having a nice time." There was no good telling her much about the other people because Mum didn't know them anyway. "There is a very big moon," she wrote, and this took her to the bottom of the page. "A girl called Rose says she will set my hair and make it fab like hers is." Then she wrote "With best wishes from Kate Lucas" very quickly at the bottom, with the curly "K" and "L" that she'd practised at school, and folded up the page and put it into the envelope and stuck the flap down tight so that she couldn't possibly unstick it again to alter anything. Now there would only be three more letters to write to Paris. She had promised to write twice a week for the first two weeks. Then in the third week she must write a "Welcome Home" letter, because Mum and Mr. Pennington would be home before she was. She would buy a postcard for Hazel tomorrow, a picture of the Esplanade and the marble steps. "Wish you were here." Hazel, swilling dried milk with her elbows tucked in, would share the wish.

The bathroom — well, she knew where it was now, anyway. But there was an odd thumping noise coming from the landing, a rhythmic jerking and panting. Someone was saying "One-and-two-and-" It was Richard's father. He was wearing shorts and a T-shirt and he grasped a pair of dumb-bells.

"Sixteen-and-hallo-and-" he said when Kate appeared in her dressing-gown. He pushed and pulled, bent and stretched like a machine. He grunted. His face was red and shiny. Sometimes he pranced, keeping in one spot and lifting his knees very high.

"How is Mrs. Blunt's headache?" Kate asked. "Richard told me about it."

Mr. Blunt put himself into neutral and applied the brakes. "Oh, nothing to worry about," he said. "She'll be as right as rain in the morning, you'll see." Then he explained, "I always have to stretch my legs before I turn in if I haven't got enough exercise in during the day," and off he went again, counting.

Miraculously the bathroom was empty and no one rattled at the door while Kate was inside. Mr. Blunt was still there when she came out; he was lying flat on the floor now, and busy as ever.

"Pleasant-and-dreams-and-forty-seven-and-" he said, and she jumped carefully across his stomach and reached her own room before she giggled.

It was only when she was pulling out some of the pieces of ivy that were caught in her cardigan that she remembered Mr. Tweedle's bottle of pills. She dug into the pockets, one first, then the other, but her fingers closed only on soft wool. The pills had gone! Somewhere on her excursion through the window the bottle had dropped out. The bottle that should be waiting on the sideboard in the dining-room for Mr. Tweedle tomorrow was lying in the bottom of the drain-pipe, or at the back of a dustbin or below the bushes. Or — and this was more likely — when her cardigan caught in the ivy and she had pulled to free it, the bottle had fallen out of her pocket and perhaps — perhaps it had landed on the wrong side of the wall, in the garden of the blind house!

It was much too dark now to attempt a return journey; clouds had thrown thick shawls across the moon. Anyhow, she had done enough climbing for one day. To lose Mr. Tweedle's bottle of pills was indeed a dreadful thing to do, but sometimes when things become dreadful it is better to stop trying and let them sort themselves out. Perhaps if she got up early enough in the morning — yes, that would be what she would do, get up and look before anyone else was awake.

She stared across at the blind house. Perhaps it was some trick of the moon sliding free of the muffling clouds for a moment, or could she really have seen what she thought she saw? Something pale that might have been a hand had moved inside one of the windows, had pulled into place a curtain that did not quite meet its fellow. She was sure she had seen it. It was a hand, it had moved, it was inside the room. Someone lived in the blind house.

Who could it be? It was all much too difficult, and her head felt thick and whirly with the need to sleep. To-morrow she would have to do some thinking: about Mr. Tweedle's pills (the Tweedles would have said their prayers long ago and be in bed by now), about the Mad Hatter and where he went every day on Aunt Poppy's bicycle and why he had stood so long at the wall, staring, and about Aunt Poppy and her worries, and about Richard ready now to walk along the high board in the bathing-pool, about Rose and Marni (what did Rose do with her hair before she went to sleep?) and about the occupant of the house at the bottom of Aunt Poppy's yard, and whether Miss Darlington had found words for the sunset after all.

She lay on her back in bed and had time only to stare for a minute or two at the bedroom walls and the ceiling, like the flat sides of a great grey unfamiliar tent. In three weeks' time she would know the shapes and slopes and angles of them all by heart.

Then she fell asleep and dreamed that the fish-bones on the worn places of the stair carpet had grown into real fish and were swimming up and down the stairs in patterns, saying "One-and-two-and-" to each other. It was surprising that they didn't bump into each other, for when she looked closely she saw that every fish was blind, they were all blind, because of the curtains that had been pinned tightly across their eyes.

⤳ 4 ⤶

SHE DIDN'T remember the moment of waking but found that she was now awake, and that her blue dressing-gown was hanging on the end of a brass bedstead instead of on the wooden bedstead where she was accustomed to find it. The sun shone through her curtains in strong yellow bands, she could smell bacon frying, and down in the yard someone seemed to be playing tunes on the lids of the bins. Milk bottles rattled, the music from the kitchen radio came up hot and hearty, there was a shuffling noise that meant ashes were being shaken down, and a voice called "Puss, puss!" — a whole orchestra of morning noises. The clock in the hall joined in. Kate counted the strokes: six — seven — eight — nine — was it really as late as that?

With a jolt she remembered Mr. Tweedle's bottle of pills. She jumped out of bed and crossed to the window. Below her in the yard she could see the broad back of Edna, who had finished riddling the ashes from the kitchen range and was now shovelling coal; she could see her aunt snatching the dish-cloths off the line very quickly, as if she had some kind of a grudge against them. Now she had rolled them up and put them into a basket at her feet and was hanging out a troop of newly-washed cloths that steamed in the morning air.

So that was that. No hope at all of repeating last night's journey before breakfast — she had slept too long and too late. Probably by this time Mr. Tweedle was seated at the table with his napkin tucked securely below his chin, while Mrs. Tweedle searched the sideboard for the missing medicine bottle.

She pulled her clothes on quickly and carelessly (jeans and a jersey would satisfy Sea View this time), did nothing to her face but wash it, and showed the comb briefly to the edges of her hair. She'd slept on it the wrong way and it was wasted work to try anything more ambitious.

Halfway down the stairs she stood aside to make way for her aunt who was coming up, carrying a big tray laden with dishes. The tray was heavy; Aunt Poppy was panting, and pausing between steps. Yes, Kate told her, she'd slept very well thank you, the bed was very comfortable. She took a quick glance at the tray, counting the cups. There were two of them. Two people were breakfasting upstairs, could it be the Tweedles? If it was, then that gave her until lunch-time to find the missing pills and put them back where they ought to be. Hope rekindled, she went down the final flight doing some fancy kicks, and was feeling almost gay when she entered the dining-room. It was as she had hoped it might be; Mr. and Mrs. Tweedle's chairs were empty and no plates had been laid for them. His dining-room bottle, Mrs. Tweedle had said; he must have another bottle upstairs.

There was no sign of gaiety from anyone else at the breakfast table. Richard stirred his porridge around but didn't seem interested in lifting the spoon any higher; Rose yawned widely and charmingly between each mouthful of toast. It seemed that she had reached the tail end of an argument with Marni and was putting the finishing touches to it.

"You do go on," Rose complained. "You don't have to talk to him, I told you. You just listen."

"That's all right provided there's something to listen to," Marni growled. "I told you — he hardly uttered a word, it was terrible. I couldn't think of anything either. What did Peter talk about?"

Rose explained that it was frightfully interesting but she couldn't remember now. She had listened but she hadn't really heard, and what in all the world had Kate been doing with her hair?

Miss Darlington was gobbling bacon. In between bites she looked out of the window. Mr. Blunt had helped himself to the last piece of toast without apology. His watch lay on the tablecloth in front of him. "Always best at the bathing-pool at high tide," he said. "That gives us an hour, just time for a quick trot along the beach beforehand, eh Richard?" Richard's face was now the same colour as his porridge. There were lines below Mrs. Blunt's eyes. "You'll exhaust the boy," she complained. "Not my idea of a holiday."

Aunt Poppy came in with a full rack of toast and the Mad Hatter helpfully took it from her and managed to spill the slices all over the table. People fished them out of sugar basins and marmalade and cups of coffee. "It's the sea air," the Mad Hatter explained pleasantly, "I don't know my own strength." He turned to Richard and asked, "Tell me, young fellow, did you ever see a bun dance on the table?" Richard gave him a glance that meant didn't the man realize he'd grown out of riddles years and years ago, but the Mad Hatter looked like a pleased dog who is waiting for someone to throw a ball for him.

"Oh come on — surely!" he coaxed. "Someone must have seen a bun dance on the table?" People munched and took no notice. "A-bun-dance," the Mad Hatter explained, saying it slowly so that everyone would see the point and be sure to laugh. With sad embarrassment Kate remembered uncles who were funny but not quite funny enough. "A-bun-dance, abundance on the table," the Mad Hatter repeated.

"How very amusing!" exclaimed Miss Darlington. "Why there's the postman, I do believe!" and she went pink right into her hair.

Edna brought the letters in and laid a long pale envelope beside Aunt Dilly's plate. She looked at it as if she was afraid to touch it in case it bit, then gulped down the rest of her coffee and said, "Excuse me," and took herself and the letter out of the room. "Nearly every morning," Marni told Kate. "You'd think she'd have got used to it."

"Got used to what?"

"I told you. Her poems. They keep coming back. I don't know why she goes on trying."

When breakfast was over Kate escaped upstairs to see what chance there was of setting off on a search party for the pills, but soon saw that there was none. Edna was seated on the back step with an apron full of green peas, shelling them into a basin. Everything that happened in the yard and beyond it would be visible to her; there was no hope of getting past unseen; and a substantial mountain of pods were waiting to be worked through.

"Be sure to remember to make your bed every morning," Mum had said, so Kate made it very smoothly and carefully, turning in the corners much more professionally than she ever did at home. This made her feel a little better. Now she would post her letter, that would be two good marks. Surely some time during the morning the coast would be clear for her to recover the pills. The important thing, she told herself, was to avoid joining forces with anyone else this morning, so that she would be free to dodge upstairs every half hour or so and find out if it was safe to go out over the roof and across the wall. It would mean a restless kind of a morning, but there was nothing else to be done.

She found Marni squatting at the foot of the stairs. She'd been putting varnish on her nails and now she was waving her hands about like dizzy butterflies. Hopefully she said, "Let's go out, shall we?"

"Just got to post a letter," Kate explained, jumping over the bottle of varnish. "Anyway your nails aren't dry yet. And where's Rose?"

"How should I know?" Marni asked crossly, while the

butterflies speeded up their frenzied pace. "She didn't tell me. Just went. Sometimes she's like that."

Kate found a pillar-box not far away. She slid Mr. and Mrs. Godfrey Pennington through the slit and heard the letter drop softly on top of all the other letters that were already waiting. That was as far as her imagination needed to take it.

Now she felt better and breathed in the morning air. You could almost taste it — not like the air at home that you never really noticed except when the wind was blowing from the soap factory. This fresh, new air gave her the wonderful idea. Why hadn't it occurred to her earlier? What a loon she was, what a bird-brain! She remembered how her cardigan had caught in the ivy on the wall and felt certain now that the bottle of pills had fallen inside the garden of the blind house. Why slide down drainpipes and hide behind bins and shin across roofs and climb walls to get inside the garden? Why not just walk until she found the gate of the blind house, and once inside she could nip through the bushes, keeping along the boundary wall, and collect what she wanted the easy way? Even if someone lived there — and she wasn't sure about that, you could think yourself into seeing all sorts of things in the moonlight — those windows weren't meant for looking out from and no one would see her.

She discovered a narrow path at the side of Sea View Guest House. Probably this would take her where she wanted to go. The ground was grown right over with

E

moss and weeds; not much traffic went this way. But at the far end of the path her progress was barred by a gate, or what had been a gate. Most gates were for going through, but this gate wasn't. Boards were nailed across it from the inside; a piece of corrugated iron had been propped there and was fastened more firmly in place by the stems of weeds and ivy; and in case this wasn't enough, a tangle of rusted barbed-wire made sure that no visitor got the wrong impression. Kate poked around to find out if there might be crawling room anywhere, but decided that even an athletic spider would have found it hard enough to reach the other side.

So that was that. She would have to revert to Plan One and go back to her lookout at the bedroom window. Perhaps by this time Edna would have finished the pea-pods. But would Marni have left her post on the stairs? Better give her another ten minutes. And perhaps she might collide with Mr. Blunt and Richard on their way to the pool, and Mr. Blunt would invite her to come with them. Richard would like that, I don't think. If she went near the guest house now she would run into all kinds of hazards. Why not wait until mid-morning when people would have decided what to do and be doing it and Aunt Poppy and Edna would be laying tables or cooking? That was the best plan. In the meantime she would just lurk about and avoid meeting any of the other people.

It was surprising how difficult it was to lurk. Doing nothing seemed all at once to be a most suspicious way to behave. The people going past with tennis rackets and towels and picnic baskets looked at her accusingly — she was sure they knew. You could be arrested for loitering, couldn't you? (Hazel's eyes would pop; it might almost be worth it.) She spotted the Mad Hatter on the opposite pavement walking with quick electric heels — it was obvious he had somewhere to go. Kate turned and stared at a string of funny postcards in a shop window until he had disappeared. The postcards weren't even very funny. She saw Mr. and Mrs. Tweedle moving gently towards a seat in the sun; they were holding on to each other as if they shared four wheels between them. Kate was consumed with guilt and stepped into the post office to buy a stamp for Hazel's postcard, but Miss Darlington was there buying stamps, probably for next week's poetic output.

Yesterday Kate had been a stranger in Sunny Bay; she could have turned cartwheels along the pavement if she'd taken a fancy and never raised an eyebrow or a greeting. But today the place was stiff with people she knew and needed to avoid.

She sought sanctuary inside one of the wooden shelters, choosing on purpose the side which the sun hadn't yet reached. There was a smell of toffee papers and damp concrete. Here she would stay until she judged the time was ripe for her expedition. It was a good place for lurking. No one would intrude on her solitude. Everyone was out collecting sunlight.

Not quite everyone. A boy and a girl had stopped just at the entrance to the shelter. It was Rose and Peter. Peter was talking.

"Did I tell you," he said, "about our dog who wagged

his tail across a plate of bread and butter so that six slices of the stuff stuck to his tail like flags?"

He told her about the dog who had wagged his tail, and about the other dog who tried to get round to the back of the mirror to attack the dog who was growling at him. "They don't usually see themselves in mirrors, did you know that?" No, Rose didn't.

"Did I tell you," said Peter, "about the gardener we had at school who had an artificial foot and one day I saw him in the potting-shed putting oil in the hinges?" No, he hadn't told her about this either.

If Kate had had the sense to make her escape right away she didn't believe they'd have noticed her, but now that she had started to lurk it was probably safer to go on lurking.

"Did I tell you," said Peter, "about the skeleton in the box that my uncle who was a doctor left in the attic in Grandpa's house?" He enjoyed telling her about the skeleton and how inconvenient it had been.

"Did I ever tell you," he asked, "about the time my little sister dyed her hair green by mistake?"

Rose said she didn't know he had a sister.

"She's loony, the things she does," Peter said, and told Rose about the green hair.

"What colour is her hair when she doesn't dye it?" Rose inquired. He said he thought it was probably brown.

"What sort of brown?"

"Just brown."

The sun by this time was edging into the entrance of

the shelter and falling on Rose's hair so that it looked like gold that had caught fire.

"Did I tell you about the school play when Juliet's hair fell off in the middle?" Peter asked. He told her about Juliet's hair and about the master at school who took his teeth out and crowed like a rooster whenever someone in the class got no mistakes in their maths exercise and how one day the Head came in in the middle of it. He told her about the boy who was hit on the head with a cricket ball and was flat out for twenty-four hours, and the other boy who lost an eye when something blew up in the lab and about his own dramatic appendix. He told her about the goat who ate the bread poultice. All these things he told her since it seemed to matter very much to him that she knew them — as if he would only be real to her when she had heard them. Rose was coiling the ends of her hair round her finger-tips and letting it go again, quickly, as if her fingers were hot.

Kate understood exactly what Peter was doing and why he was doing it. She'd been doing much the same thing at home during the last few months with the person she was trying to remember to call Uncle Godfrey and must now find a new name for. "You see, when I was a little girl I couldn't say 'Hospital' properly, I always said 'Hostipal' . . . you see, when I was a little girl I had measles and learned to play the recorder while my eyes were sore and Mum counted how many times I played 'Sur le Pont D'Avignon' and —" "Yes," Mr. Pennington had said smiling and still obstinately Mr. Pennington, "Yes, I see. How very interesting." "You'd like to see her form photograph, wouldn't you, Godfrey?" Mum asked. Kate showed him the photo. None of the girls looked real or interesting, not one. They were all dummies.

"Did I tell you about our science master, the one we called Isaiah?" Peter asked. "Well, you see, he was our form master and he did the marks every week and he used to divide us into grades when he read them out. The ones at the top, the real brains, he called them Super Heroes, and the ones below that he called Heroes, and the ones below that again he called Stout Lads, those were the pretty average types, and the ones below that, the duds, he used to call them Fishballs."

"Why Fishballs?" Rose asked, looking very beautiful, and Peter said he didn't know really, that was just what he'd called them.

"Let's go down the pier, why don't we?" Rose said. "Lots of people are there already."

"Did I tell you," asked Peter as they moved away, "about the time my aunt went to sleep in a telephone kiosk?"

Now the coast was clear for Kate. Time she was getting back to base if her plans were to succeed. She kept her eyes dreamy and faraway, not seeing properly, the way she practised doing during lessons as a source of private entertainment when she knew that otherwise she would just fall apart with boredom. And so, moving quickly and bumping into people who were shapes and couldn't possibly be anyone she knew, she reached the guest house unchallenged.

Richard was in the hall. He had his back to her and didn't turn round. All right, that suited her, she could nip upstairs without having to talk to him.

But she didn't. Curiosity hooked her before she reached the stairs. It was the way Richard was standing, slap up against the row of coats and mackintoshes and other belongings that hung from hooks against the wall. He was stuck there as if he was growing roots, staring at the belts and sun-hats and shrimping-nets and dog leads and string shopping-bags and waterproof hoods the way he might stare at a Western just at the moment when the Goodies have pulled their socks up and decided to win. He was pretending, of course. He wasn't really seeing any of them, they didn't matter. They just gave him a reason for being there and that was what he needed. His bathing-togs were wrapped round his neck. His hair, she noticed, was dry.

"I thought you were going to the pool," she said.

He didn't move or turn round. "I was. I've been."

There was an empty moment. Kate felt embarrassed and wished she'd gone upstairs after all. "Look, I'm sorry," she faltered, creakily.

"Don't strain yourself."

"I only said I was sorry."

"I know. I heard."

"You were all right last night. I saw you. Twice you did it."

"So what?" Richard snapped. "Today I didn't, not even once."

"Why?"

He turned at last and she saw how white and sick his face looked. "You tell me. Go on — tell me."

"Didn't you explain to him about last night at the rocks? You could have told him."

"Fat lot of use that would have been, I don't think."

"Did he say anything?"

"I wasn't listening."

"You must have been listening."

Richard didn't answer, just turned back again to stare at the row of coats. Kate said, "Well, you've still got three weeks, haven't you?" and he laughed, an odd croaking kind of a laugh, and said, "That was just what he said, if you really want to know."

Kate was sorry for him and at the same time indignant because she had to be sorry. It was inconvenient at that moment to spend time being sorry for anyone, except perhaps for herself. And with things the way they were, she might have to go on being sorry for him on other mornings. The idea struck her coldly. It would be as bad as Aunt Poppy's tiredness and Miss Darlington and the postman. It was a mistake letting yourself get tangled up with other people. There had been a poster on the wall on the way back from school — a girl in a bathing-suit looking beautiful and solitary and thinking beautiful solitary thoughts, lying stretched out on the sand, everything gold and blue and empty except for the girl and the sea. Underneath was written "Get right away from it all! Be your own lovely self!" "There you are — that's you at Sunny Bay!" Hazel had sighed enviously, thinking of the crowded inches of the family caravan and all those elbows.

But it didn't look as if things were working out that way. Mr. Tweedle's pill bottle was still waiting to be recovered — that was bad enough. And here she was now stuck with being sorry for Richard. Meanwhile the clock pointed to half-past ten; faint hints of tomato soup and sounds of cooking were already seeping through from the kitchen passage. The rest of the house was quiet, no sign of anyone. This was the time to get moving — she must act at once. The sea and the sand and the beautiful thoughts would have to wait.

"Where's your dad?" she inquired.

"Filling up with ozone."

"And your mum?"

"Resting again. Her head came on."

"Where's everyone else?"

"Out."

It occurred to Kate that since she seemed to be collecting worries she might try adding one worry to another and see if that made one worry less. Richard's misery plus the problem of the missing bottle of pills might cancel each other out — or at least one would shrink the other.

"Look," she said, not allowing herself time to think about it in case she changed her mind. "I've lost something. I have to find it before lunch."

"Why don't you get on with it, then?" Richard asked sideways without even a flicker of concern.

"It's Mr. Tweedle's bottle of pills."

Richard gave a rude hoot of a laugh and said, "Is that all?" and Kate felt cross and pranced as far as the stairs. All right, let him be miserable. Then she stopped because Richard added, "You were a nit. Where did you lose them?"

So she squatted down on the stairs and began to tell him the whole story through the banisters, about how she had put the pills in the pocket of her cardigan last night when Mrs. Tweedle asked her to return them to the dining-room, how she'd gone climbing out over roofs and walls the evening before, how she'd nested in the ivy to avoid being seen, how she'd almost overbalanced.

Halfway through the recital — she was describing the difficulty of shinning up the drain-pipe on the return journey — it struck her that telling Richard all this was a horrible mistake. He hadn't been able to go off the high board at the pool this morning — here she was letting him know how clever she'd been at drain-pipes and roofs, how it didn't matter to her that so many yards of empty air gaped between the soles of her feet and the ground. That would please him no end, I don't think.

"So you see when I got back into my room," she said, regretfully skipping all mention of her skilful manœuvre across the window-sill, "I found that the bottle wasn't in my pocket any more. It must have fallen down on the other side of the wall."

Richard evidently hadn't taken any offence. He said,

"Well, why not go and have a look for it, why don't you?" and she felt relieved and started gabbling about how difficult it would have been this morning with Edna parked at the back door.

"You are a prize loon," Richard said and she agreed yes, she knew about that.

"Actually," Richard said, "I'm going into the yard now, if you want to come."

"You're what?"

He was unwrapping the towel that was swathed round his neck. "That's where I hang up my togs to dry," he said. "On one of the lines down at the bottom."

The music of brass bands struck up inside Kate's stomach. "Oh, Richard!" Perhaps she was behaving like a baby getting a present off the Christmas tree, but she didn't care.

"Are they wet?" she asked, and then went hot all over because this wasn't the most tactful of questions. Luckily Richard didn't seem to notice. "You wait," he said. "They soon will be," and he went up the stairs two at a time.

She heard the water running in the bathroom. When he came down he was grinning. "Come on then if you're coming," he bade her. His togs dripped pleasantly on the linoleum all down the passage to the kitchen.

Edna was there, busy over a range crammed with saucepans. She didn't turn round. There was no sign of Aunt Poppy.

"Just going into the yard to hang up my things," Richard announced, and Edna snatched a lid off a white froth of milk and made noises that meant let him get on with it, why bother her?

So they were through the kitchen door and in the yard. It had been as easy as that. Kate felt inclined to giggle, but there wasn't time. They found a space on one of the clotheslines and Richard hung up his togs. Then they went on through the wilderness of bushes, by unspoken agreement squatting down so that no one looking out from any window would see. No sense in inviting people to be interested.

They reached the wall. By morning sunlight it looked tame and easy, not the mysterious ivy-swathed height that she had scaled in last night's moonlight. There was a door in the wall but it was locked; they would have to climb it anyway. Child's play, she thought meekly, allowing Richard to select the best place for an assault. She followed him up and squatted beside him. Torn strands of ivy showed her where she had made her previous roost.

"Here! It was here!"

She needed just one more miracle and because she was so sure she was going to get it there it was. Probably this was how you did miracles, by being sure. Through the tangle of leaves and stems on the top of the wall, the white label of the pill bottle showed up plainly, the pills like miniature green Easter eggs. The bottle hadn't fallen through the ivy to the ground — she had only to put her hand down and pick it up.

"I've got it."

"Hang on to it this time."

There was no need for him to tell her that. She pressed the hard glass into the palm of her hand to consolidate the miracle. Things had come out right after all. She felt buoyant with bliss and morning sun. Any minute now she might just float off the wall in sheer gratitude.

Richard was rootling about in the ivy muttering unhappily to himself. "All the way to the pool I knew I was going to do it, I was quite sure. I didn't even go in for a swim beforehand. I went straight up the ladder. And then suddenly I knew I couldn't. It was no good trying, I just knew. And when I came down there were some kids waiting. They ran up the ladder like monkeys and took off, laughing all the way down until they hit the water." He stared over at the blind house. "Queer sort of a place. I heard them talking about it last year when we stayed at the Splendide. The owner of the Splendide wanted to buy it, to extend. He was dead keen. He wanted to buy Sea View as well — they said he'd offered a big price but Miss Lucas wouldn't sell."

"I don't suppose she would," Kate said feeling indignant, but surprised to find herself taking sides for Sea View against its glossy neighbour.

Richard was still gazing with interest across the wall. "A right mouldy old dump. I never got a proper look at it before. I used to wonder what it was like."

Kate felt a prickle of danger and said quickly, "It's just an old empty house."

"Whoever owns it, they wouldn't sell."

Kate said: "I'd better nip back and put these pills

where they belong," but she wasn't quick enough. Richard had already said, "Let's go across, why don't we, and explore?"

All at once the sun seemed to grow colder. "Don't let's bother."

"Why not?" He was looking at her; he knew why not, he didn't have to be told. This was something he wasn't afraid of and he was going to show her. He would enjoy her being afraid. It was her turn.

"I don't want to. There isn't anything to see. And anyway —" But he was already halfway down on the other side of the wall. She stowed the bottle in the deep pocket of her jeans, it would be safe there, and followed him uneasily, telling herself she should have had the sense to stay where she was. Hot uncomfortable fear ran right through her. A long branch reached out and grabbed at her hair and cheek.

"We shouldn't. We shouldn't, really."

"I don't know what you're on about," Richard said, "and you've scratched your face, it's bleeding." She sucked blood and wished he wouldn't talk so loudly. If she had to be here, surely the place demanded tiptoe and whispers?

"Come on!" Richard was already on his stomach and writhing through jungles of untended shrubbery. Reluctantly she followed. For some distance she saw nothing of him but his heels. Then the shrubs thinned a little, Richard's feet were drawn forward into sunlight, and soon she too was standing upright, staring.

They had reached a clearing and were now on what

74

had once been a lawn but was now grass as deep as a meadow, matted with the uninterrupted growth of many summers. There was nothing except a different level of greenness to distinguish paths from lawn. A few ragged spikes of colour showed where flower-beds had been. A wooden trellis that had collapsed offered a wilderness of roses. On the crooked roof of a summerhouse dandelions were thick. The supports of a swing leaned together; the seat was coated thickly over with moss. One of the ropes had almost rotted through; probably it was the spiders' webs that prevented the last threads from parting.

Richard was hauling at some netted cords which the grass had almost swallowed. "Anyone for tennis?" he shouted, capering. "Don't, Richard, don't!" The fabric snapped in his hands and he fell over into the grass still laughing, laughing longer and louder because now he knew for sure she was scared.

"I wish you wouldn't. I wish you wouldn't," Kate muttered, hating him. It wasn't only that she was afraid. This place had been a home — there was no need to mock it now. People had been happy and busy here; no one should laugh like that. Probably no one had stood where they were standing, no one had laughed, for years and years, and when they did it had been a different kind of laughter. She felt ashamed of Richard, and of herself for being with him.

They were now very close to the house, but the muffled windows offered no challenge. There was a conservatory on this side of the house. Some of the glass panes were broken, but the curved ribs were intact and gave the place an air of elegance. Weeds grew into it and through it and from it, finding no difference between inside air and outside air. The door from the garden into the conservatory swung unlatched.

"It's open," Richard exulted. "Come on, what are we waiting for? Let's explore."

"No, I can't." She dug her feet deeper into the grass, wishing she could take root. "I just can't."

"Why not, for any sake?"

"Perhaps the place isn't empty. We can't go prancing in as if we owned it."

"Of course it's empty."

"You can't be sure."

He smiled in a lordly way and said, "We can make sure."

To reach the conservatory door they had to step high over the fallen branches of a monkey puzzle tree that lay like the scaled body of a serpent. Once inside, broken glass grated in the weeds below their feet. Richard closed the door behind them. Inside there was a stifling reminder of elderly ferns and long-decayed geraniums, there were watering-cans and seed-boxes thick with dust. A pair of stilts were propped against a wall. Beside it was a doll's house, the little chimneys entwined with greenery. Kate forgot she was afraid and stooped to look inside, then straightened uneasily.

Glass doors from the conservatory opened directly into one of the rooms of the house. The panes of these doors were uncurtained. Kate grabbed at Richard's arm

76

and was then frozen right through by fear. Inside the streaked glass something had moved.

Richard had seen it too. He stood stock-still. The movement had been arrested but the pale shape was still there. Inside the room someone was standing looking at them. After a long moment the pale shape moved slowly away.

"It's all right," Richard said at last, and there was a wobble in his voice. "Whoever it was he's gone now. And let go of my arm, can't you?"

Richard was right. When she found courage to look steadily through the glass there was no one there. She exploded into anger. "What did I tell you? You are a prize idiot! I said someone might live here. You had no business to come barging in, I told you, didn't I? Laughing the way you did like a crazy hyena. And I'll tell you why, it was because you knew I was scared, that was why you did it, wasn't it? You liked me being scared, you were showing off because you weren't scared, did you think I didn't know? Making a fool of yourself, stampeding through other people's houses —"

She would have gone on much longer, but Richard without warning took hold of her shoulder and shoved her down among the weeds and glass on the conservatory floor. He held her there, whispering savagely, "Shut up, can't you? Someone's coming!"

She was too startled to object, and now she could hear the footsteps for herself. They came from the garden, a quick, muffled tread. Someone was crossing the grass. The steps came closer. Now the door of the conservatory

F

swung open. Someone was standing there, but didn't enter. Instead, an arm was extended and a basket was set down on the floor not far from where they were crouching. Then the door was pulled close and the footsteps retreated.

Richard's grip slackened. Slowly they stood up, staring at the basket and at each other.

"Did you see who it was?"

She nodded. They had both seen. It had been Aunt Poppy.

"How do you suppose she got in?"

They went stealthily as far as the door of the conservatory and watched. Now Aunt Poppy was picking her way back over the grassy prairie. Now she had disappeared into a gap between bushes.

"There must have been a path after all. We should have looked for it."

"That door in the wall, that's how she came."

"It was locked, idiot."

"Then she has a key."

"Let's get out of here."

"Not yet. Give her time to clear off first."

They looked at the basket on the floor. It contained parcels of groceries, a packet of biscuits, some apples, a bottle of milk. So that was it. The drama and the danger evaporated. It was all as plain as daylight. "Whoever lives here, your aunt does the shopping for them," Richard jeered. "Some dotty old hermit!" No mystery, just an old person who lived alone and Aunt Poppy did the shopping. There was also a folded bundle of laundry.

"His washing! She does his washing, too. That's all." Kate felt cheated and a little foolish for having expected anything else.

At last they judged it was safe to go. When they opened the door of the conservatory a piece of paper that had been tucked between two of the parcels was disturbed by a draft of air and blew out into the garden. Kate retrieved it and brought it back.

"Better read it, hadn't you?" Richard mocked. "I expect it's in code. Aunt Poppy's a Secret Agent, we ought to have known. Funny the things you don't notice even when they're right under your nose."

"Don't be silly," Kate snapped. "It's only a grocery list." There was no need for Richard to go on like that. She crumpled the scrap of paper and stuffed it into the pocket of her cardigan to show him how unimportant she knew it was.

They recrossed the grass quickly. Yes, there was a narrow path between the bushes — Aunt Poppy had gone that way. If they'd scouted around they'd have found it themselves. It led them to the door in the wall. When they tried the door it was locked, as they had expected it would be. Richard climbed the wall first, scolding all the time.

"All that mystery," he said, "all that sprawling about on roofs in the moonlight. The sort of game kids play, getting ourselves scratched to bits worming through bushes because we didn't take time to look if there was a path. Fine pair of loons we were. Scared of some silly old man who looks out at us through a dirty window — or do you suppose it was a death ray? Well, go on — was it? We ought to have tested the butter for radio-activity! You watch too much telly, that's your trouble! And you'd better nip back quick and put those pills where they belong or Mr. Tweedle will collapse and breathe his last into his tomato soup and his blood will be upon your head for the rest of your days!"

They went through the yard and into the house without speaking. Edna was counting spoons and didn't look up. Kate put the bottle of pills thankfully back on the sideboard in the dining-room and went upstairs to her room.

She smiled unsteadily at her reflection as she tidied her hair. Boys were like that. She pulled off her cardigan. The scrap of paper inside the pocket rustled and she took it out and smoothed it on the dressing-table.

It hadn't been a grocery list. The words that were written in Aunt Poppy's handwriting were: "He says he must see you."

⤙ 5 ⤚

"A THEFT in a saucepan," pondered Mrs. Tweedle, with her pencil poised over her crossword. "Seven letters." She looked round inquiringly but no one could stir even a flicker of interest. They were much too hot, much too happy, much too lazy.

"A theft in a saucepan — come on, someone!"

"Has it got something to do with the Knave of Hearts?" the Mad Hatter suggested from below his tilted hat.

"You don't make tarts in a saucepan," Mrs. Tweedle told him kindly, and the Mad Hatter said, "Oh, but I do, I always make my tarts in a saucepan — before I put them through the mincer, of course."

It had been like this for four days, but already it seemed there had never been any other kind of weather. You expected the sun to be halfway up a blue sky when you looked out of the window in the morning and there it was, pale but hot. By the middle of the morning it had climbed to the top of the sky and was scorching, too bright to look at. All afternoon the sunlight never blinked or faltered, there wasn't a trace of a cloud. Even the long yellow blazing sunsets were hot, even the nights, with nothing but a single sheet over you, and your toes and knees and elbows making peaked mountains in it, like egg whites whipped thick.

The Tweedles were encamped on the stretch of beach beside the big black rocks that stood like a family of paddling elephants halfway along the bay. Rose and Kate and Marni had joined them. It was too hot to go any farther. Mr. Tweedle was swathed in rugs and his wife had propped a large umbrella over his deck-chair, as if he were some kind of Eastern potentate. The girls divided their time between the warm sea and the warm sand and trailed their hands and feet in the pools that the receding waves had scooped at the base of the rocks. Richard came up and squatted beside them but didn't talk.

"No diving practice today, then?" Mr. Tweedle inquired.

Richard avoided Kate's eye and confessed that he had a spot of ear-ache.

"Nasty thing, ear-ache," Mrs. Tweedle said, and tilted the umbrella an extra couple of inches towards her husband's head.

Rose spread a towel and oiled herself and lay like something in bronze out of the Art Gallery except that she turned over every half hour. Her aunt Miss Darlington was extended in a deck-chair. She looked very warm and ecstatic and breathed sunlight in a purposeful way to let everyone know she knew she was doing it. The Mad Hatter sprawled full-length on the sand, one knee bent and the other lying across it, so that his legs made interesting spiked shadows. Every ten minutes or so Mr.

Blunt went by, prancing gently, and they waited for the air to cool down again after he had gone.

"Poached," Mr. Tweedle said suddenly.

"What was that, William?"

" 'A theft in a saucepan' — poached."

"Oh, how clever you are!" Mrs. Tweedle licked her pencil and filled in the word. "Poached! So it is! So easy once you've got it! Poached!"

"Eggsactly," the Mad Hatter said solemnly.

He had been like this all morning, just funny enough to raise a comfortable giggle, not so funny that you had to clutch yourself and roll about. It would have been too hot for real laughing. Kate felt the heat pressing her into the sand. She kept her eyes closed but even inside her eyelids it was fiery. She was sticky with sand all over. In a little while she would flop into the warm sea and wash it off, and then come back to the beach again to watch the salt dry in white patches on her arms and legs. It was too much trouble to unscrew the bottle of Bronze Bloom.

This kind of weather excused her from thinking. And she felt comfortable now with these people who had been strangers five days ago. This morning someone had rattled the bathroom door before she had finished and she had called "Righty-ho, then!" without hesitation or embarrassment. It was almost like being in a family except that if you wanted to you could get up and walk away and be separate. In a family, even if you walked away you couldn't be separate. And all that drama about the blind house and the hermit, all her wild speculation over the words that were written on the piece of paper

— "He says he must see you" — probably it was someone to mend the telly or a man about the drains. It wasn't as if it mattered. The only things that mattered were the sun and the sand and the sea.

Mrs. Tweedle wrote another word into her puzzle. Rose turned over again. Kate opened her eyes to watch her and noticed that Rose's eyelashes were now a paler gold than her cheeks. What did Rose think about? You never knew. Or did she think? If you looked like that you mightn't need to think very much. Marni was a violent raspberry pink, peeling right into her hair. She gave Rose a look of warm envy and asked Kate what she was doing this afternoon.

"Doing?" Why should anyone want to do anything?

"I thought we might do something," Marni suggested. "Go somewhere."

"Where, for instance?"

"Oh — anywhere."

"Aren't you going out with Mike?"

"Why should I?" Marni pushed her hand into the sand and lifted it so that the dry grains poured off slowly, giving her fingers a webbed appearance.

"Is he still dumb?"

"Who?"

"Mike."

"Oh — him!"

"Anyway, aren't you going out with Rose?"

"She's going to wash her hair. Anyway, she says she's right off boys."

"Even Peter?"

"Peter?" Marni looked as if Peter was someone out of the Lays of Ancient Rome. "No. That's all folded up ages ago. There's still Edgar, of course."

"Edgar?"

"A boy from home. She's dotty about him. Anyway, let's go somewhere, you and me. Gosh, I feel like a boiled pudding or something."

"Where'll we go?"

"Oh, anywhere. We can decide later on."

Lunch at Sea View was calamitous — very thin slices of luncheon meat and warm wisps of salad. Aunt Poppy was valiantly cheerful but looked exhausted. Mrs. Blunt pushed the salad round her plate as if she was haymaking and said no to the bottle of mayonnaise. Afterwards it was creamed rice and apricots and Mr. Tweedle took his pill. Miss Darlington missed the only chocolate biscuit on the plate and didn't seem to notice.

Marni was lying in wait in the hall afterwards. She captured Kate and they set off along the Esplanade. In spite of the heat Marni seemed in a hurry, determined to explore but hard to please. She said no to the pier, no to the Dodgems, no to the swimming-pool, no to the Hall of Mirrors, no to the Fortune Teller, no to the Talent Spotting. "We might meet people," she explained, speeding past the glossy snack bar, and looking carefully at all the people she might meet, to see who they were. Kate was getting hot and cross. "Where will we go, then? Make your mind up."

They had come to the far end of the Esplanade. There wasn't much more to choose from. Outside a sad-looking tent a notice said, "THE KOOKY KAPERS KON-CERT PARTY — Twice Daily — 3 o'clock and 7:30. Home-Baked Melody and Fun." A man at the door was taking money and a few grown-ups were going in, flat-footed, carrying peppermint creams and knitting-bags and folded newspapers.

"Come on. This'll do," Marni said. "I'll pay."

When her eyes had adjusted themselves to the dark-ness, Kate was able to make out a small stage and rows of chairs. The audience was sparse; nobody except them-selves seemed to be under forty. She felt like asking Marni if she was sure this was a good idea, but since Marni had paid for both of them it might appear rude to be doubtful. On the stage a piano was playing. She thought it was a tune Mum used to sing but she couldn't remember its name. Then the curtains parted and the show began.

Something in the pit of her stomach told Kate it was going to be terrible, and it was — right from the begin-ning. There was a lady who sang, her voice swooping up and down like a swallow, and all the time she was sing-ing she smiled, so that the song emerged spikily from the edges of her teeth. There was also a gentleman who sang about an English Country Garden. This went on and on, always the English Country Garden. You knew when it was coming and waited for it. The pianist had dark glasses and a red beard. In between songs he got up and was funny. He played on an accordion, coaxing the ladies and gentlemen in the audience to join in. Most of them did. They sang "Tea for Two" and "A Room with a View" and "I'll See You Again".

"Now boys and girls, let's get really good marks for this one," the pianist said, and they sang about Roses in Picardy. Some of the audience took off their spectacles afterwards and wiped them on their hankies.

The lady and gentleman came in together and sang about the Keys of Heaven. Another lady danced, holding some flowers and wafting them about. The pianist got up and was funny again. It was the turn of the gentleman to sing.

> *A woman, a woman, oh what can she be?*
> *Whatever she is, she is nec-ess-ar-y!*

He danced and his knees made cracking noises.

It was when the pianist got up to be funny for the third time that Kate was quite sure. Up till then it had only been a vague notion of a ghost of an idea that ran round inside the top of her head, something she nearly imagined but hadn't any words for. He was playing that tune again, the tune Kate thought she'd recognized at the beginning of the programme, and there was something about the way his long hands flopped about on the keys, stroking the tune out of them, something about the shadow his head threw on the curtain behind him. And when the tune was over and he began to be funny again — then in one silent, private thunderclap — she knew! Underneath the phoney B.B.C. accent which now and then slipped a bit (by mistake on purpose) into a raw cockney she recognized the voice of — the Mad Hatter! The Mad Hatter's eyes were behind those dark glasses, that red bristling beard concealed his chin!

For a moment she felt nothing except a warm shame that threatened to drown her. Perhaps Mum did sing that tune, but it was also the tune, the little coaxing tune that the Mad Hatter had played on his recorder on her first evening at Sea View, when she had opened a door hoping to find the bathroom and he had closed it gently with his tadpole-covered socks. This was where the Mad Hatter went on Aunt Poppy's bicycle! This was what he did with his afternoons and evenings! He was a Kooky Kaper. His was the "Home-Baked Fun" in this crummiest of crummy programmes. This morning, while he was spread elegantly on the sand, putting a gentle word in at just the right place, she had loved him warmly. And now here he was!

The first lady had come on to the stage again and she was singing:

> *Dear little jammy face, I love you so.*
> *You're just the very idol of your Mammy.*
> *I loved your Daddy, dear, long years ago*
> *And all because his little face was jammy!*

Toffee papers were rustled appreciatively among the audience. The lady sang the verse again while the piano played an agile hopscotch in and out of the words.

Kate by this time was sticky all over with embarrassment. Marni hadn't uttered a word. Perhaps she hadn't realized who it was behind the red beard and the dark glasses; she didn't seem to be registering very much of what was going on, just scratched at her sunburn absent-mindedly and seemed to brood. Kate had expected a critical elbow in her ribs or a groan of disgust in her ear long before this, but there had been neither. All right then, if she hadn't guessed for herself she wasn't going to be enlightened. Kate decided that this was a sorry secret she would keep to herself.

The ladies and gentlemen came and went and at last the performance was over. They were standing on the stage in a row, holding hands, bowing and smiling. The pianist blew kisses out of the thickets of his beard and said: "Cheery-bye, cheery-bye till the next time, all you lovely people!" and then the curtains closed across them.

Without any warning Marni became alive. "Come on — let's get back!" She pushed like a terrier and they beat all the mums and dads to the exit.

The Esplanade was packed solid, prams two abreast on the pavement, battalions of buckets, spades and shrimping nets, the air noisy with Crisps and twined with Candy Floss. All the way back Marni didn't say a thing, not one single lament about the Kooky Kapering. Kate wondered if she was expected to say thank you, but couldn't get enough enthusiasm worked up. Anyway, Marni had seen for herself what it was like. If it had been Old Fashioned Music Hall on the telly, with the audience dressed up in velvet and feathers, like Christmas cards, it might have been excusable, but there they had been — real people in hair-nets and sandals, cotton frocks or shirt sleeves, not acting as if they were enjoying themselves but really enjoying themselves! It was something Kate wanted to forget about as quickly as she could. Better not give Marni a chance to say what she thought. To help even things up Kate suggested an ice-cream — she would treat. But Marni wasn't keen, she just skipped like a flea through the crowds, looking everywhere, at everybody, as if she were taking the Register.

Suddenly there was Mike, standing a few feet away. Marni stopped.

"Hallo."

"Oh, hallo, Mike!" Marni said in a "fancy meeting you" kind of voice.

"I was looking for you."

"Oh, were you?"

"Yes."

"I was out with Kate. We had a simply super afternoon, didn't we, Kate?"

Fortunately Mike didn't give Kate a chance to reply. He said: "I wondered where you were."

"I told you. Out with Kate."

"I looked on the pier but you weren't there."

"No. I wasn't. I told you."

"I didn't see Rose, either."

"Didn't you?"

"I went to the pool and looked." He described other places where he had looked, and Marni agreed that she hadn't been there either. Meanwhile in front and behind them a traffic jam was building up on the pavement; people were jostling, prams trying to manœuvre, dogs on leads doing a bit of Maypole dancing. Kate tugged at Marni to come on but she didn't seem to notice.

"I just wondered where you'd got to," Mike said, and Marni said, "I was with Kate," and then they both dried up. But somehow they drifted off in the same direction, the dogs, prams and people unwound themselves on the pavement, and Kate was left standing by herself.

She was in a bad mood before she reached Sea View, and the letter on the hall table didn't improve it. The writing seemed to jump out at her and catch hold — guess who's here! Her own name written in Mum's writing on the envelope with the foreign stamp. She had been waiting and ready for a letter at breakfast this morning, but there was none. Miss Darlington hadn't got a letter, either. Here was a letter now, and Kate wasn't ready for it. During this first week the sharp edge of newness had worn off, things that happened at Sunny Bay were now more real than things that might be happening in other places, remembered or imagined. Home and Paris had been lying nice and quiet in her imagination, and now this letter had come to interrupt all that.

She carried the letter upstairs and sat on her bed for a while before she opened it, trying to accustom herself to the idea. It's only a letter, people get letters all the time. It was still only a letter when she had read it. It didn't say very much. Mum was having a wonderful time, she was sure Kate was having a wonderful time. The weather in France was beautiful, she hoped the weather at Sunny Bay was beautiful. Paris was a lovely city, the buildings and the shops were lovely, Kate would love them. Uncle Godfrey was very well and sent his love ("Of course he's not 'Uncle' now, is he?"). Kate was to be sure and give Aunt Poppy her love. And then "With love from Mum" written at the bottom, with the same squiggle under the words that was always on the labels tied to Christmas presents and on the notes left on the kitchen table telling her what was in the fridge for tea and how much bread she was to take when the bread man called.

As soon as Kate had finished reading the letter, the room in which she sat became foreign ground. The walls and the windows and the wardrobe were all wrong; it was the wrong pattern on the curtains. These things weren't just wrong, they were unreal and hostile. Home was the only real place.

She thought of it now passionately and remembered it in detail. It was a little house, built of brick in a row of little brick houses, but there was something about its ordinariness that made it dear and different. Her bedroom was at the back, the window looked out on the canal that ran at the bottom of the short gardens. Sometimes the light, reflected off the water, threw shining pools of wetness on the ceiling. Sometimes the water in the canal steamed because the soapworks farther upstream were discharging hot water. There were always swans on the canal, slow, clean, unsociable birds. On the far side of the canal rose the three tall factory chimneys and the squat shape of the gasworks, and in the distance the five mysteriously-curved cooling towers, grouped like a committee of presiding gods. The electric pylons strode across the skyline.

Mum's room was across the landing, at the front. Her dressing-table stood in the window, with the photographs on it, and her hair-spray, and her bottles of nail varnish, and the heart-shaped china box with flowers on the lid. Downstairs there was the front room and the back room and the kitchen spreading out into the garden. There was the lilac tree that had to be cut back every year to make room for the clothes-line. There was the procession of round white stones marching round the bed of ferns. They had brought the stones back with them from a holiday, it had been Mum's idea to put them there. Kate thought about all these things, remembering each of them carefully.

The clock struck, announcing that tea was almost ready, but she didn't stir. She heard people coming up the stairs, but didn't try to guess who they were. She heard the bathroom door opening and closing and the water gushing through the pipes. The smell of sausages stormed across the window-sill. People were going downstairs now; she heard them laughing.

Presently Edna knocked and put her head in and asked if Kate was coming down to tea, so down she went. Everyone was very cheerful and jolly, as if to redeem the dismal lunch. There were plenty of jokes, and Kate was filled with indignation because they could behave like that, because her own sadness didn't matter to any of them. The Mad Hatter was sitting opposite her. She avoided looking any higher than his now beardless chin.

G

Aunt Poppy said, "Aren't you eating your sausages, Kate?" It was the heat, someone said, and Mrs. Blunt agreed that hot weather was like that, one hadn't really an appetite for sausages, had one? Kate's sausages grew stiff on her plate. Mr. Tweedle took his medicine. Mr. Blunt dug his knife into the cheese. Miss Darlington wondered what the chances were for a good sunset. "Aren't you eating your trifle, Kate?" Aunt Poppy asked. It was the heat, Kate explained.

She went back to her room afterwards and sat there without putting on the light, still counting things over in her mind, as if she were picking them up and collecting them. Twice somebody rattled at the door but she pretended she wasn't there. Once, because it was Marni who called, she nipped inside the wardrobe to avoid being interrupted. It mattered very much to go on with what she was doing until everything had been counted and remembered. The door opened and closed again. Inside the wardrobe Kate nearly giggled. Then Marni's footsteps went quickly downstairs, like a pack of skil·fully shuffled cards.

Kate came out of the wardrobe and went to the window, but she didn't see the blind house or hear the music from the Splendide. It would soon be dusk. The swans always came upstream as soon as the sun was fading — they swam grandly as if they were in a procession when really there were only three of them. The sky was very faintly pink above the cooling towers.

Much much later, when the house was quiet and her collection was complete, Kate went downstairs armed with coins, because she was now very hungry. There would be a slot machine somewhere, she could collect enough to stop herself from feeling empty. It had been a pity to waste the sausages and the trifle.

The Mad Hatter was coming up the steps as she went down them. The evening session of Kapering was over; now he was returning home. He hooked his arm into Kate's and wheeled her round and they came down the steps together.

"I'm hungry," he announced. "We're both hungry. That's the worst of bangers, it's all over so quickly." She laughed obediently and waited for him to go on about how it had only been a trifle to follow, but he didn't, and she blessed him for being content to leave that joke out.

The fish bar was crowded but they found a table. The fish was beautiful, white and hot and juicy, crisp with breadcrumbs. The lemon juice stung her tongue. Every chip was a separate pleasure. The tea was thick and strong. She felt comforted through and through, outside and in.

"I was silly at tea," she said.

"Sillier than usual?"

"You know I was."

She had finished the last chip, the final shred of fish. He asked her what she would like next. She had been debating this in her own mind. The menu in its plastic holder stood between them on the table. Frooti Tooti or Knickerbocker Glory, she hadn't decided yet. You don't often have the choice between two Happy Endings.

"Come on," the Mad Hatter insisted. "What'll it be?"

She had the uneasy feeling that he too had been studying the menu and that the hand that moved inside his trouser pocket was exploring to see how much money was there. Perhaps this was only her imagination. Grown-up people normally have plenty of money for things like fish and chips and ice-cream. You didn't have to be careful. She had never yet aspired to a Knickerbocker Glory, it was the ultimate, and she would be able to tell Hazel. But Frooti Tooti sounded more exotic, and there might be nuts as well as fruit. They both cost the same. Frooti Tooti it would be!

The coins in the Mad Hatter's pocket clinked between his fingers. It was unfair and embarrassing. The Mad Hatter had a habit of being larger than life and then a little smaller, so that being with him was a succession of enthusiasms and disappointments.

"Make up your mind," he said.

"I hate making up my mind."

"So do I." She remembered his face as she had seen it in the moonlight from her perch in the ivy. This decided her. Self-denial was a sad business, but necessary. "I won't have anything else," she declared. "I couldn't, honest. Not another bite."

"Sure?"

"Quite sure."

His hand came out of his pocket. She tried not to think that he looked relieved.

They walked back slowly. The lights were lit along the Esplanade but the enchantment had gone out of them. Tonight they looked cheap and artificial.

"Let's go down to the edge of the water and walk across the sand," the Mad Hatter said. "The tide's on the way but we can come back by the Esplanade."

The incoming tide was already halfway up the sand. It was lonely and beautiful here on the edge of the water. The illuminated sea-front seemed a long way off and the lights were toy lights. Here the waves were real and the sound of them was the only sound. The sea had work to do, it was in a hurry. It fell on the scuffed and untidy beach, flooding the moats that the children had dug during the day, toppling the proud gate towers, blunting the parapets, swamping the castles. Each wave took the work of destruction a stage further. Fortifications soon became sad little humps. Houses which had been so stoutly built, with decorations of shells and elaborate seaweed gardens, lost all their identity and were just a stain in the breaking confusion of water. Whole towns were consumed as the tide marched up the beach.

"No time to waste," the Mad Hatter said, taking her hand. She had to match her stride to his long steps.

"Was it right what Richard said — people have been drowned?" she asked, already out of breath.

"Yes." She felt his hand tighten. They reached the far end of the beach and climbed up a flight of steps to the Esplanade. They sat down together on the sea-wall. Kate felt safe and happy. She recovered her breath. Now she wanted to talk. He was the right person to talk to.

The day before she came to stay at Sunny Bay had been the day of the wedding. In the morning she had packed her case and had taken it round to Mrs. Higg's house next door. She was to stay there overnight because there wasn't a late train to Sunny Bay. "It'll be nice for you, staying with Mrs. Higg, won't it?" Mum had said. "She'll put you on the train in the morning."

"Go on," the Mad Hatter said.

When she came back from leaving her case next door, the taxi came to drive them to the wedding. "This the lot, then?" the taxi man asked, looking at Mum's cases, and Mum said, "Yes, that's the lot," and the man carried them down the path. "Slam the door for me," Mum said, so Kate slammed the front door and they got into the taxi to take them to the Registry Office.

So after she had waved Mum and Mr. Pennington off to the airport Kate went round to Mrs. Higg's house. Mrs. Higg's house used to be interesting and exciting because all the things in it were opposite to the way they were in her own house, like in *Through the Looking Glass*. Mrs. Higg was very kind. She looked into Kate's room on her way to bed and sat on the edge of the eiderdown and talked.

"I'm going to miss you and your mum next door after all these years," she said. "It's been a long time. I remember the day you were born, your dad came round to tell me." And she said, "It'll be a lovely house you're going to out on the Estate, you'll be very grand living out there, won't you, dearie? Just think of coming back to a new house like that! Great style, so I'm told, out on the Estate," she said. And she said she'd do everything she could to make it easy for Mum when she came back from Paris at the end of the honeymoon and moved her furniture out of the house next door.

Kate said she wished she could be there for the move, but Mrs. Higg said, "Better not, dearie, and look at the lovely holiday you'll be having at the seaside with your auntie."

That night after Mrs. Higg had gone away Kate didn't go to sleep for a long time. She was thinking about the other room in the other house just through the wall from her room in Mrs. Higg's house. The other house was empty now, nobody in it at all.

"Go on," the Mad Hatter said.

Kate tried to explain. "You see, I just walked out of our house that morning without even thinking. And I won't be going back. I didn't remember it would be the last time ever. You see, when they come back from Paris they'll be living in the new house on the Housing Estate. But I just walked out and slammed the door. 'Be sure and give it a good hard slam,' Mum said. She couldn't slam it herself because she was wearing white gloves and because of her flowers. She was excited and smiling. 'Go on, slam it,' she said. So I slammed it. I should have remembered. Last times are important."

"There'll be the new house," the Mad Hatter said. "First times are important, too."

"It wasn't even a very special house, the old one," she went on, vexed with herself because she minded so much. "There wasn't really anything you'd call special about it; it was just part of a whole row of houses."

He said, "Any house you've grown up in is bound to be a special house."

She hoped this rare, comfortable conversation could go on for a long time. She felt peaceable and easy sitting there on the sea wall with her shoulder against him, and her feet scuffing the concrete path when she swung them.

He said, "Tell me about the house," so she told him about the little strip of garden at the back and about the swing, and how when she swung high enough she could look over the fence and catch a glimpse of the flat shining waters of the canal. When he'd swung high enough in his garden, the Mad Hatter said, he used to be able to see the lighthouse, and in the evening he often matched the swing to the flashes, timing it perfectly, up — down, on — off! There were swans on the canal, she told him. Seagulls coming in to roost in the fields behind the town, he said, great slow birds.

She told him about the lilac tree and how it had to be cut back every year because its branches drew sooty lines across the washing, and because the leaves kept the sun off the row of lettuces. There was a monkey puzzle, the Mad Hatter remarked, a huge absurd joke of a tree that grew right across the croquet lawn. It should have been cut back regularly but it never was. Sometimes the branches of the lilac reached as far as the bicycle shed, Kate said. "The Dump," that was what they called the bicycle shed. It was always bulging with all kinds of things besides bicycles — anything there wasn't room for, that's where it was dumped. Families were like that, the Mad Hatter agreed — things got dumped any old where that was convenient.

"Like putting a doll's house in a conservatory," she said, without giving herself time to think. It was now the Mad Hatter's turn to speak but he didn't. He wasn't looking at her, he was staring straight ahead with a peculiar expression on his face. She wasn't sure whether it was because he thought she was talking nonsense, or whether what she had just said made such unexpected and excellent sense. Curiosity niggled. "I kept my doll's house upstairs in my bedroom, and when I was too old for it it was given away to the hospital. 'Well, you don't play with it any more, you're too old for it,' Mum said. 'There isn't any sense in keeping it when you don't play with it.' "

If she went on talking long enough he would have to say something, wouldn't he? So she persisted. "She can't have played with it for ages, can she? It was thick with dust and spiders' webs and the weeds were sprouting out of the chimneys. Anyway I suppose she's grown up now. It must have been years and years since anyone played with it."

"Twenty-five years or thereabouts," he said.

"Then she is grown up?"

"No," the Mad Hatter said. "She's dead. She was drowned." And his long arm scooped her off the wall and set her in the direction of Sea View.

~⟨ 6 ⟩~

"KEEP STILL," Rose directed smoothly. "How can I do a thing with you leaping around like that?"

"I wasn't leaping."

"You were."

There was no chance of leaping, but neither was there anything to be gained by arguing about it. Every hair on Kate's head felt as if it was being tweaked individually. Her scalp prickled, the smell of the setting lotion made her eyes smart, there was a crick in her neck, a small spiked worm must be boring tunnels inside her forehead. She'd been an idiot to allow herself to be let in for this performance, but she hadn't had much choice. Rose had taken charge as soon as tea was over and had lured her to the dressing-table. Already the operation seemed to have been going on for years. Kate's face, fringed by rollers, stared back at her glumly from the mirror. It reminded her of something pale on a plate, an offering trimmed with sausages. Rose, whose reflection appeared fleetingly on either side of her own, was still serene and maddeningly beautiful, though she had forgotten about it and wasn't trying. This was additionally unfair. Marni sagged on the bed, twiddling at the transistor, and sometimes offering advice.

"It'll be dreamy when I've finished, you'll see," Rose promised.

"If it ever is finished."

"Not long now," Rose said.

"It better not be long," Marni complained, wriggling. "The fireworks start at eight."

"You're getting a spot, did you know?" Rose reported. "No, two spots." She harvested a lock for the next roller. Her comb made white lines across Kate's scalp, and another hundred hairs that Kate had forgotten about woke up and took notice. Kate, in whom all pride and ambition had long since died, felt sorry for her face, as if it were something separate from her. Poor old thing, you don't half look silly!

"Golly, I'm hot!" Marni turned over and flopped on her back, lying with her mouth open like a fish. They were all hot. It had been hot all day, but with a different kind of heat. There wasn't enough air around, even in the shade. The sky had been streaky since morning, and now in the late afternoon there was a peculiar orange light that was almost solid, lying like syrup over everything. Even at the water's edge at midday there hadn't been the ghost of a breeze. Toy boats were becalmed, toffee papers lay where they fell, dogs sprawled and panted, the waves collapsed without enthusiasm or purpose, there was no loud-voiced colony of scavenging gulls.

"It isn't going to rain, is it?" Marni rolled towards the window. "It couldn't rain, not tonight."

"Rain?" They hardly remembered in this sun-hot

world what rain felt like — it was as impossible as woollen underclothes and frosted windows, chilblains and Christmas decorations.

One of the rollers on Kate's forehead lurched forward and exploded; the lank wisp of hair began to uncoil. With maddening good nature Rose twisted it up and secured the roller again.

"We'll never be ready in time," Marni said edgily. "What time did you say we'd meet the boys anyway?"

Rose's eyebrows were raised. "Boys?" You'd think she'd never heard of boys in her life. Boys? Would someone explain, please?

Marni yelped and hauled herself upright. "You mean you didn't fix it with Peter? You said you would."

"Well, I didn't. Not anything definite."

"Why ever not?"

Rose shrugged. "Oh, I don't know, it didn't seem worth fixing an exact time. I just told him we'd be around."

"If it had been Edgar you'd have said what time," Marni accused, and Rose agreed, yes, of course she would, but it wasn't Edgar, was it?

Marni groaned and made faces in Kate's direction, inviting her to take sides. Kate didn't want to be on anybody's side and held her tongue. Marni snapped and snarled, Rose went on with the hairdressing. Rose was a mystery. What sort of things did she mind about? You never knew. Kate held her breath and waited for the next yank; her eyeballs were now sticking out like gooseberries.

It hadn't been a good day in the guest house. There was a kind of peppery irritation in the air. People seemed prickly and separate, nobody was able to settle down to do anything — as if nothing was worth the bother, but doing nothing was equally unsatisfying. This morning there was no contented assembly on the sand. The guests had wandered about avoiding each other, writing postcards to friends whom they knew a lot better than the other people at Sea View, who had somehow shrunk to strangers. Nor had Kate got any further with her own private problems, the blind house, the words written in Aunt Poppy's writing on the piece of paper, the Mad Hatter's affairs into which she had intruded in so puzzling a way. What was she to do about any of them? It was a silly question, she decided. Whatever was going on had been going on before she came, and nobody had asked her to do anything. Her brain was numb, though conscience and curiosity were still uncomfortably lively.

Tea had been a difficult meal at which unfortunate things had happened. The chips were soggy, the rissoles bled when a fork pierced them. Edna streamed with a summer cold; Mrs. Tweedle had noticed and was sending out an invisible smokescreen of imaginary disinfectant round her husband. Halfway through the meal Mrs. Blunt got up without comment and walked out. At the end of the table Aunt Poppy's face reddened slowly, then went gray. Mr. Tweedle didn't want any apricots, thank you, dear Miss Lucas. Miss Darlington was hardly interested in her plate; she was still haunted by the two long envelopes that had lain there at breakfast. The Mad Hatter sagged and was squeezed dry of jokes. Mr. Blunt, with his muscles creaking impatiently, reminded Richard that the tide in the pool would be at its best around midday next day, they mustn't miss the chance must they, and Richard had laid his spoon down and looked across the table and said, "Just as long as I don't funk the high board this time," and then nobody else said anything until Mr. and Mrs. Tweedle asked a blessing. Certainly one was needed.

Now Marni had developed hiccups. The springs of the bed vibrated. "Oh, those rissoles, they were terrible!" She clutched her stomach and bounced. Kate got the message, you couldn't very well miss it. Sea View Guest House was a second-rate establishment; Aunt Poppy tried but she didn't try hard enough; people came here because they hadn't been able to book in anywhere else, or because it was the only place they could afford.

"Aunt Poppy works very hard," Kate said, wondering if her face could redden with her skin stretched as tight as it was now, "and she's had a lot of experience."

"Well, of course she has," Marni said with careful nastiness. "Even before she had Sea View she was a housekeeper, wasn't she?"

"Yes," Kate said. It was the first she'd heard of it, but how could you say that all you'd known about your aunt until a month ago was a box of handkerchiefs at Christmas and a book token on your birthday and sometimes a picture postcard. Aunt Poppy had earned her living by being a servant, what was wrong with that? Marni was only going on this way because she was too hot and had hiccups and was angry with Rose. Anyway, did you have to be on the side of your relations just because they were your relations? "She does her best, you can't say she doesn't."

"I daresay, but she's getting past it, that's what," Marni said. "You'd think she'd know she was past it and give it up." Now she was scolding Rose again. "You ought to have fixed a time. There'll be thousands of people in the park this evening. Suppose we miss them?"

"I don't see it matters all that much if we do," Rose said, maddeningly pleasant. "Anyway why don't we just go on our own, you and me and Kate?"

"On our own?" Marni couldn't believe it.

They argued while Rose secured the final roller and began to do expert and interesting things to Kate's face. Nothing Kate had ever done to her face was like this. She watched her face changing into someone else's face. "There, that's that!" Rose said at last.

Marni heaved herself off the bed and she and Rose competed for the other mirror, still squabbling sideways at each other. Kate wondered why Marni bothered to go on about it. Rose would win. Marni ought to know that by now. Rose would always win.

Now Kate wasn't hearing them any more. She was looking at herself in the mirror. Suddenly she knew that this moment had become important, a moment for always. This isn't someone else's face looking at me. This is my face. This is what I'll look like in twenty years when I'm old like Mum is. It was frightening, but exciting. This is my face grown up, showing what it wants to show, knowing the answers but not telling them. I'll remember this, the first time I saw myself grown up, the first time of all. It was like looking at a photograph that hadn't yet been taken — but it was a good photograph. I'll remember this, this room and the hot evening and the scenty smell and the dull voice of the sea, the traffic outside and the pompitty-pom of the brass band just starting up in the park and the other two yapping at each other and me here, sitting at the dressing-table suddenly grown up and ready to go out to see the fireworks. I'll remember this the first day of term when I put on my school uniform. "Tallest on the right, shortest on the left and no more talking." A lot of kids, all eager and giggling and obedient. But I'll remember this.

Fireworks used to be great fun, Dad striking matches down at the bottom of the garden, getting his fingers burnt and swearing, Mum laughing and clapping her hands as the Roman candles rose into the air, ball after ball, Kate herself perched on the fence so that she could see the red and blue and yellow reflected in the canal — "twice as much value for the money," Dad said. Gunpowder had an intriguing smell, faces appeared for a brilliant moment as the flame of each match lengthened and grew steady; sometimes after a rocket faded and died you could hear the soft plop of the stick falling into the canal. The clock in the town-hall tower was striking nine. "Somebody'll be sleepy in the morning," Mum said.

She knew that this moment in front of the mirror was

an important first time, and she understood now why Rose hadn't made any firm arrangement to meet the boys. It would be far more glorious tonight to walk out, Rose and Marni and herself, arm in arm across the pavement, united and laughing and self-sufficient. If they felt like noticing any boys they might notice them. Other people were going to notice Kate and Rose and Marni. "Look at those girls arm in arm! Look at them laughing! Look at the one in the middle!" Rose would be in the middle, nobody would argue about that.

Rose had now completed her own preparations; she came to take the rollers from Kate's hair and brush it out. Kate tried hard not to look, not to hope or expect. When finally she did look it was almost past belief. The girl in the mirror smiled at her, eyebrows and mouth curving in pleasure. The next time she smiled it was wider and better. "I told you you'd look fab," Marni said. Kate didn't dare to answer. If Hazel could see her looking the way she looked now! Poor old Hazel, devoting the evening to the pursuit of Mrs. Dose, the Doctor's Wife! The third time Kate smiled she tried looking mysterious and fascinating on purpose and it worked. It had never worked before.

"Come on then," Rose directed. "What are we waiting for?" This evening they weren't waiting for anything, the evening was in attendance on them. They went downstairs smoothly and magnificently. Miss Darlington was standing in the hall, licking down an envelope. She said: "Going out together to the fireworks? Well, that's nice!" Aunt Poppy, still grey and harrassed,

H

went along the passage and said, "Going out together, that's nice, isn't it?" before she disappeared into her room. The Mad Hatter was setting off for the evening's Kaper. "Well well well!" he smiled. "All dressed up and somewhere to go!"

They came down the steps of Sea View abreast, arm in arm with Rose in the middle, and joined the parade to the park. Everything and everyone was going in the same direction — their direction. (Kapering would be thin business tonight.) The soft oompa-oompa of the band took its time from the girls' feet. The lights on the Esplanade blossomed at their approach. The fireworks were waiting for their personal enjoyment. The evening was theirs. They were three young Queens who had graciously decided to walk to their Coronation instead of travelling in their golden coaches. Kate could see that Marni on Rose's other arm was happy now, and quite content with things the way they were. Apparently she had done some private arithmetic and got the same wonderful answer. Who wanted to hang about waiting for boys? This was much more splendid, just Rose and Marni and Kate.

Already a great many people had gathered in the park. The girls reached the wide open lawn where the faces of the crowd made a pale circle along its edge. "Oh — do you think we'll get places?" Marni twittered, but Rose smiled and they got places all right, slap at the front.

Now, because they had arrived, the band worked itself into a frenzy of welcome and delight, drums rolled, cymbals sliced the air apart, the excitement had become almost too much to bear. There was a final fanfare of brass, a final flourish of the drums, the cymbals spoke, and then, in the succeeding silence and without any warning so that it took your breath away, a whole colony of rockets carved their way up into the sky in unison, and in unison curved and slowed, dimmed, faded and died.

Breathing from that moment became difficult because it had to be worked in in between gasps, and there was barely time even to gasp. A legion of Roman candles was dispatched and carried everyone's eyes up above the dark fringe of the bushes, where against the sky whole galaxies of coloured worlds were launched and shot softly upwards. Gold and silver snakes writhed and crackled along the ground. A stupendous bang took the crowd by surprise, the air was filled with pungent smoke; now another rocket tilted all heads skywards, separating stars from fireworks. Catherine wheels spun in their thousands.

Then in the dimness impossible things happened. A clown made all of lights danced across a tight-rope twirling a sparkling umbrella, a Cheshire kitten made a leisurely entrance and smiled, jewelled birds were hatched from invisible nests and flew away into the shadowy retreat of real trees. A fountain of silver water poured continuously and fish swam in and through it, keeping perfect time to the beat of the soft waltz which the band was playing.

The smell of gunpowder and trodden grass was now agreeably mixed with the smell of cigarette smoke and perfume, of chocolate and the first dew falling on the bruised leaves of the shrubbery. In the summer evening the make-believe world had become real. Kate's knees were weak with joy, her throat ached with a kind of tender delight. The brilliant pageant went on as the darkness deepened. Now any magic was possible, marvel followed on the heels of marvel. There wasn't time to be taken by surprise and yet the whole evening was a procession of amazements. Each amazement made Kate hungry for the next. Go on, go on. It couldn't go on like this.

It didn't. Somebody's shoulder was against hers and was pushing. She moved an inch but the shoulder followed. It was Peter. He said, "I wondered where you were," and looked over Kate's head at Rose.

Kate didn't answer. She wished he would go away; he would spoil it all, would break the spell. This beautiful enchantment was something to be enjoyed privately, person by person, it wasn't anything that you needed to share. Peter was still staring at Rose; a toppling cascade of splendid purple rain fell into the tops of the trees and was wasted on him.

Rose had caught sight of Peter. "Tell him to go away," she whispered fiercely. In case he had heard and was offended Kate turned towards Peter and smiled. The smile of course was a mistake. She had intended it to be a friendly smile, a kind of "She's only being funny, don't mind her" smile, but apparently it had worked out mysterious and fascinating. Peter unhooked his eyes from Rose and fastened them on Kate instead.

Now what had she done? Any other time it would have been a triumph, but not now. "Their eyes met," that was what it said in the stories in Mum's magazines. So that was what it was like! They'd met, all right! A reluctant thread of excitement tightened in her stomach. What could she do now? She couldn't say, "Look, that was a mistake, that smile, take no notice of me, it's only my face, Rose has been glamming me up." You had to be careful how you smiled when your face was the way it was now. Perhaps it was funny, but she didn't think so. What a time to choose for her first success! There must be some way of unsmiling without being rude. "Is he still there?" Rose said sideways.

He was. He was glued on like a leech. At Kate's elbow he was holding a non-stop while-you-wait life-story. He talked his way through a shower of orange and green butterflies and a lively fusillade of fairy cannon, through a picture of the Queen in red, white and blue, and through a miraculous bush that grew and budded in the night sky and burst into leaf and flower. Kate swallowed hard on her fury and tried not to hear him. It was her own fault. That would teach her to smile.

"Our science master at school, he was awfully keen on making fireworks, he used to let us have a go in the lab sometimes, did I tell you?"

"No."

"He made a mistake once and blew off the top joint of his little finger, as neat as anything it was, did I ever tell you about that?"

"No."

In front of them a fairy palace was rising into the air, mysteriously erecting itself, storey after storey. Towers and turrets sprouted, domes swelled, and from the top of the highest tower a long silky banner shook itself free. The crowd gasped and cheered.

"He was our form master," Peter explained, "the one we used to call Isaiah. He did the marks every week and he used to divide us into grades when he read them out. The chaps at the top, the real brains, he called them the Super Heroes, and the ones below that he called Heroes, and the ones below that again he called Stout Lads, those were the pretty average types, and the ones below that, the duds, he used to call —"

Kate had become desperate. "Fishballs," she said smartly. She heard a snort of astonishment. When she looked round Peter was edging away with a deflated expression on his face. Rose had heard what had happened. "Good for you!" she commented smoothly.

Kate pushed Peter out of her mind as best she could. She felt ashamed at her own rudeness though a little elated at its success. You could do this, it was easy. She waited now for the spell of the evening to fall on her again. A fresh burst of light screamed up into the sky. "Ooh — ooh — ooh!" breathed the crowd as their heads lifted. "Aah — aah — aah!" they exclaimed as the points of gold and silver were dispersed and fell away into darkness. Then, from the fringe of the crowd at the farther side of the ring, there came a mocking echo — "Aah — aah — aah!" cleverly and deliberately making a joke of the enchantment.

Someone laughed, and from that moment the evening was destroyed. On the edge of the spectators, on the side farthest from where they themselves were standing, Kate could see a group of leather-jacketed boys, mostly with crash helmets swinging from their hands. They were big fellows, the showy type. They were restless. They'd had enough of this kids' stuff. Children's Hour had gone on too long, it was time somebody broke it up. Now there was more laughter and a scuffle. A squib had been thrown; it crackled noisily among the feet of the crowd and was stamped into silence.

That finished it. The crowd had already forgotten about the fireworks and remembered themselves, standing there with their mouths open, gawping, like children at a pantomime, believing in the magic. How infantile could you get? Magic? Fireworks were something you bought in a shop. They were bored with fireworks, they were waiting for something more lively to happen.

They hadn't long to wait. The next squib was greeted with treble squeals and more laughter.

Not everybody was pleased. Here and there a voice was raised in protest. "Shut up, can't you!" "That's enough of that!" "Clear off!" Someone was talking through a loudspeaker. "Now then, ladies and gentlemen, now then, if you please. I'm sure none of us want anybody's high spirits to spoil the evening for the rest of us, do we?" The gang thought this was very amusing and raised a cheer. Some of the men from the spectators, heavy young fathers most of them, had stepped into the open arena and were moving in the direction of the disturbance. Behind them mothers held back screeching children. Squibs were thrown at the men as they advanced and there was some nervous laughter. Above the trees a coloured fan of fireworks spread itself unnoticed.

"Please, please, that's enough of that," the loudspeaker entreated, but nobody paid any attention. There were other things to claim their interest. The men came on slowly, sizing up their opponents.

Kate was excited in a way she had never felt before. At the beginning she had been indignant with the gang for wrecking the lovely evening, but now this hot excitement filled her and dried up her throat. She clenched her hands, digging her nails in hard, and waited to see what would happen. "Silly young idiots, only out for trouble," said a man who was standing at her back. With her whole heart she hoped he was right, she ached for trouble. She was on the side of the boys, she wanted them to win. She heard herself cheering when another handful of squibs was thrown.

She enjoyed the novelty of feeling this way. Any other time if there was even the smell of trouble she would have run a mile. She was always the scared one, ask Hazel. Drunk men, for instance, even men who were only feeling festive and chatty — if one got on to the bus Hazel had to sit on the outside because Kate was frightened. Even with her school hat on Hazel could deliver a suitably crushing bit of repartee while Kate just got red and giggly with embarrassment. Sometimes on the way home the boys from the Comprehensive started up a fight and began to punch each other and throw things. If

Hazel wasn't with her, Kate would go back and walk home the long way rather than edge herself past them. But she wasn't frightened now. She heard a woman cry out, "Stupid no-goods!" and longed to bellow a contradiction. Someone said, "It could get rough!" The rougher the better!

The men who had detached themselves from the crowd were now nine or ten yards from the troublemakers. The boys had closed their ranks and were waiting for them. Perhaps it was their long hair and the exuberant clothes they were wearing that gave them a dramatic quality, like people in history. The crowd was silent now and watching. All attempt at continuing the fireworks had been abandoned. The music from the band ambled half-heartedly on with The Gold and Silver Waltz, but soon this faltered and broke and whined into silence. The voice on the loudspeaker had stopped bleating.

It was quiet enough now to hear the tread of the men's feet and the dogged breathing. From the ranks of the boys one boy, taller than the others, had stepped forward. You couldn't help noticing this boy, his height, his light silky hair, his air of authority. Pleased with himself? All right, so he should be, looking like that. What was Rose on about now? Her fingers were digging into the soft part of Kate's upper arm like hooks. Kate tried to shake her arm free but found she couldn't. Anyway she wasn't feeling her arm any more, the excitement crowded out all other feelings. It wouldn't be long now, not very long.

The thunder took them all unawares. Perhaps it had been growling around over their heads, obscured by the noise of the fireworks and the music. But now without warning lightning cracked across the sky. The men and boys ducked instinctively so that the moment of assault was lost. The lightning made a mockery of the pretty antics of coloured gunpowder and lit the whole scene with vivid metallic violence. It drew caricatures of men and trees, caricatures which appeared for a brilliant moment and were gone before the thunder broke, peal after peal.

After that came the rain. It attacked them with a solid weight and fury; the noise of it on leaves and grass and on the heads and backs of the crowd was like gasping breath. The crowd broke and fought, looking for any kind of shelter. The men in the arena stood their ground for a moment, rain already darkening the soaked shoulders of their jackets. The boys hesitated. Their wet faces and hair gleamed in the next lightning flash. Then they were off, running, stumbling, raising their arms to keep the rain from blinding them. The men made no attempt to follow, but turned to help their families to any protection from the rain's onslaught, anywhere that was dry, if there could be such a place in this drowning world. There was a crash and some screaming as one of the wooden frames on which the fireworks display had been mounted sagged and toppled over in sodden confusion. It dragged another frame down with it.

Rose still held fast to Kate's arm. "Come on," Kate urged, tugging. "Let's get out of this." Rose didn't answer or move. "Come on!" Kate scolded. Rose didn't seem to have heard; still she took no notice. Kate turned to look at her. "What's the idea?" she cried. "I'm drowned already!" With her free hand she rubbed the water out of her eyes and stared.

She had never seen Rose like this, she could never imagine Rose could look as she did now, fierce and alive, eyes blazing, standing there while rain turned her hair to seaweed and streaked her make-up — Rose, magnificent, not even remembering to think about her face.

"Did you see?" Rose demanded.

"See what?"

"Did you see who it was?"

"What do you mean? Let go of me!"

"But did you see?"

Still Kate couldn't shake herself free. Rain ran behind her ears and down her neck. What a place to choose for a conversation! Rose hadn't even noticed. Whatever it was that she was going on about mattered. Something had happened which made Rose mind, and mind badly!

"It was Edgar," Rose said. "That was Edgar!"

"The boy in the front with the light hair? Do you mean him?"

"Of course!" The way Rose said it frightened Kate. That was Glorious Apollo, surely you recognized him? You must have seen, it was Cliff, Ringo, Tom Jones.

Now from the paddock beside the park gates there came the din of motor-bikes starting up. The din increased and sharpened, then altered as the bicycles turned into the main road with a flourish, and finally diminished and was gone.

Rose said: "They've gone," and her fingers slackened. Her face was white. Marni on the other side was clucking like a hen. "Come on — come on home!" She took Rose by the hand as if she had recently suffered a severe bereavement.

They made their way as best they could, but it was difficult going. The crowd had now turned all its attention to seeking home and shelter. Children swathed in waterproofs tripped and wailed, parents tugged, hoisted, scolded, comforted and encouraged, girls with their heels stuck in muddy grass or floundering in puddles pulled off their shoes and went splashing past in their stocking soles, older women skidded, screamed and were hauled to safety. The rain fell steadily, then eased for more lightning, more thunder, then fell again.

All along the Esplanade the string of coloured lights was reflected on the wet pavements, so that they were walking in many-coloured puddles. The flowers in the urns had been battered and lurched crookedly, spilling petals. Rows of newspapers which had been laid out for sale along the sea wall were turning to pulp. Litter baskets dripped. Lightning seemed to rise from the sea and fall back into it. The waves appeared blunted and crawled flat against the sand.

Stumbling at last, drenched and shivering, up the steps of Sea View they collided with Miss Darlington who was stationed at the top. She was swathed in dripping plastic from head to foot and carried an umbrella and a notebook. Kate thought for a moment that this was the anxious aunt come to look for her nieces, but it was apparently the poetess in action, for she nodded absent-mindedly as the three girls squelched their way past her into the porch, murmured "Superb, superb!" and then stepped out a little farther to enjoy the next thrust of lightning.

Inside the hall, enjoying the dry air around her, it occurred to Kate that perhaps she should report her return to Aunt Poppy. Rose and Marni had already gone upstairs, Marni still murmuring comfort, but Kate walked down the passage and knocked on her aunt's door.

There was no answer, no sound at all except the drops of rain falling steadily from her clothes. She knocked again. She could see that the light in her aunt's room was lit. She hesitated, then turned the handle and went in.

"Aunt Poppy — it's me, Kate — I'm back!"

Aunt Poppy was lying sideways in her chair. But for the support her desk gave her she would have fallen. Her face was grey and peculiar, her eyes were closed but her mouth was open, and she was breathing in a noisy, unnatural way. In front of her lay a confusion of papers, money, envelopes.

"Aunt Poppy!"

Aunt Poppy didn't move. Kate, shocked and startled, turned and dashed back to the hall. The front door swung open and the Mad Hatter came in. He shook his hat, and the rain from its brim drew lines across the floor.

He smiled at Kate and mopped his face on his handkerchief, then removed his glasses and polished them; his unspectacled eyes blinked at her mildly. "Did you swim," he inquired, "or did you manage to thumb a lift on the Ark?"

She grabbed him by the arm. "You must come. It's Aunt Poppy. She's ill."

He put his glasses on unwillingly, as if it would have suited him better not to be able to see her too clearly.

"You must come at once. She's in her room. I found her."

He followed her to Aunt Poppy's room. Her aunt hadn't moved. Saliva from her mouth was falling in a thread on the papers below her hand.

"You can see — she's ill!"

He was looking at Aunt Poppy with that soft, useless expression on his face, distressed but asking to be excused. Kate would have liked to have been excused, she was never any good at illness, ask Hazel. It made her feel funny. Illness in an adult was additionally difficult — to touch a sick person made her numb and awkward. The Mad Hatter was still standing there, just looking.

Kate was angry with herself and with him. "Go on — do something, why don't you?" she cried. "You can see she's ill. She's tired out, that's what. All the worry of running the guest house and making it pay and people complaining and her getting older and having to be pleasant to everybody all the time — she could sell it, you know, Richard told me someone had asked her." Beside the desk she saw the basket which Aunt Poppy had carried to the conservatory on the day when she had been hiding there with Richard. There was a key lying in the bottom of the basket.

"And trotting backwards and forwards running errands for whoever it is who lives in the blind house —"

"The what —?"

"That's what I call it, the blind house, the broken-down old house at the back," she explained impatiently. "There's someone who lives there and she does the shopping for him and his washing, some dotty old hermit —"

"She was his housekeeper," the Mad Hatter said, "for thirty years."

"Until he decided to be a hermit and chucked her out so now she looks after him for free." It was surprising and exciting to discover what you could say once you'd got started, almost like hitting someone. "Why did he shut himself away from other people, anyway? What right had he got?"

But the Mad Hatter had lifted the telephone and didn't answer.

≈⟨ 7 ⟩≈

MISS DARLINGTON flung salt liberally across her bacon and egg and declared: "Give me the naked fury of the elements!"

No one answered. After last night she could have them and welcome. "And may I trouble you for the mustard?" she added, and the mustard was passed. Now perhaps she'd be satisfied and would keep quiet.

It was a vain hope. Ever since she had appeared at breakfast, Miss Darlington had entertained her companions at the table to a flash-by-flash report on the thunderstorm as if none of them had seen it for themselves. Apparently she had stayed at her post on the steps of Sea View until the last flicker, the final rumble. She was afraid those faint hearts who had hurried indoors might have missed some of the best bits.

"Your poor aunt," she said to Kate. "Undoubtedly it was the storm that upset her. I believe some unfortunate people are affected in that way."

Aunt Poppy was upstairs in bed. The doctor who had visited her late last night was coming again this morning. Breakfast had proceeded remarkably smoothly with Edna and her sister Evie (rustled up overnight from no one knew where) in command.

Kate's head still ached from last night's excitement, and her throat was hot and tickly. When she had reached her room she had been too tired to rub her hair dry and her pillow this morning was still clammy. There had been no mystery or fascination in the face she saw in the mirror when she got up, just the same old arrangement of a pair of eyes with a nose in the middle and a mouth below, the one she'd have to go on looking at for the rest of her life. Marni and Rose were pecking at their food and for once conversation had dried up between them. Sometimes Marni looked sideways at Rose in an anxious kind of way — she was maintaining her Mother Hen act of the previous evening. Rose looked like something in Greek Tragedy, or straight from the fridge. Mrs. Blunt hadn't appeared at breakfast (thunder affected her headaches), and Mr. Blunt and Richard had found nothing to say to each other. Not once had the Mad Hatter glanced in Kate's direction; there wasn't a glimmer out of him, not a hint of a glimmer. Even when he asked Edna to fetch more butter he said nothing about bringing it forth in a Lordly Dish, like he'd done every single morning till this one. So Miss Darlington met with no interruption to her ecstasies.

Kate, munching without appetite or interest, longed for the meal to come to an end so that she could get away by herself, as far away as possible from all these people. If only the postman would arrive and bring Miss Darlington today's rejected poem. That at least might put an effective sock to her babblings and clear the last of the thunder out of her hair.

I

"Sublime on the towers of my skiey bowers," Miss Darlington explained, "Lightning, my Pilot, sits," and the Mad Hatter said, "Really, how very interesting," and the postman came up the steps.

There was a letter in Mum's writing with the French stamp conspicuous on it. Now she'd have to open it with all of them sitting round watching her. There were far too many people and they were much too close. When she got back to school next term the first homework essay would be "My Summer Holidays", the same as it always was. Kate had planned to write a beautiful romantic piece with lashings of the curious way-out adjectives that the new English mistress fell for. The greedy seaweed, the crawling feathers of the waves. She intended to spread out her private thoughts for the Upper Fourth to marvel at and admire. "I wandered, lonely as a cloud" was to come in somewhere. But she could give up that idea. Who said clouds were lonely? Lonely? With all those other clouds sharing the sky with them so that they bumped into each other every couple of minutes! Who said you could have any private thoughts at a seaside guest house, jammed elbow to elbow with all the people whom you hadn't met ten days ago, and whose faces and problems and jokes and taste in toothpaste and fried eggs you now knew as well as you knew your own.

And all these people mattered, that was what made it worse. Did the Mad Hatter remember how rude she had been to him last night? Was Richard going to be able to go off the high board this morning? What would she say to Peter the next time she met him? What was the doctor going to say when he came back at lunch-time to visit Aunt Poppy? Why had a glimpse of Edgar had this extraordinary effect on Rose? Behind the curtains of the blind house the hermit at this moment was eating his solitary egg untroubled and unaffected by anything except himself. He didn't have to mind or feel guilty or worried or anxious or even inquisitive about anybody or anything. Nobody's elbow dug into his ribs, no one breathed reproachfully down his neck. She envied him.

She was comforting herself with the thought that an account of the thunderstorm would take two whole pages in the letter she was due to write to Mum this morning when from Miss Darlington's side of the table came a peculiar croak. The postman had brought her a letter too. She had opened it and it was lying beside her plate. Miss Darlington's face was pink; she was holding on to the edge of the table as if she needed to. Her mouth was open and she smiled in an uneven kind of way and said, "Oh dear, oh dear, oh dear!" over and over again.

Mr. Blunt asked, "Not bad news, I hope, Miss Darlington?" She gulped and seemed to have to search around for words. "Oh no, not bad, not bad at all," she finally fluttered. "Actually, it's just one of my little verses, it appears to have found favour in the sight of the editor!"

The news came like a belated thunder-clap. "Really!"

"How perfectly splendid!"

"Well, it is encouraging of course." Miss Darlington had gathered the letter up in her hands carefully, as if it were a flower. She was steadier now, her face was almost beautiful. "So very kind," she said, acknowledging the flurry of congratulations. "Just a few lines, you know, a random thought, nothing very profound or momentous." She rose and pushed back her chair. "Excuse me, won't you?"

Marni objected. "But your breakfast, Aunt Dilly! You've hardly started it!"

Miss Darlington looked down at the succulent orange eye of her egg and at the crisp pinky brown frills of bacon without any real interest. With her letter clasped to her blouse she leaned across the table towards her nieces. "My dear girls," she said, "I hope that as life unfolds for you, you may find it as rich and rewarding as it has been for me!"

Then like a Duchess who has opened all the Sales of Work in the world she swam out of the room. Everyone watching her knew she was going to cry when she reached the hall. They were awed, and grateful to her that she made it in time.

Embarrassment now flowed round the breakfast table in a sticky tide, lapping at everyone. They went on with their toast and passed each other the marmalade. They felt better after Edna had come and removed Miss Darlington's neglected plate. Now, in a moment, someone would find the right thing to say and they would all be easy again and comfortable.

This might have happened if it hadn't been for Rose. She stood up suddenly and her face went red. Marni pulled at her but Rose pushed her away. She banged both her fists down on the tablecloth so that the tea-spoons jumped in their saucers. "How could she say that to me — to me!" she cried, and didn't notice that she had tipped her cup and that the steaming tea was spreading a stain steadily across the table. With loud insulted sobs she followed her aunt out of the room.

There was an empty moment before Richard asked, "What do you suppose she was on about?" Marni gave him a scalding look and yapped, "Of course you wouldn't understand, how could you?" before she in turn went in pursuit of Rose. Richard sighed noisily and said, "Girls!" and Kate, who was inclined to agree with him, allowed the insult to pass.

It was soon plain that the remaining adults at the table were going to do nothing to redeem the awfulness of what had happened. Mr. Blunt mopped at the pool of cooling tea as if it was the only thing that mattered. The Mad Hatter scraped at his already scraped plate; you could tell from his expression that he was yearning for a red beard and dark glasses. Kapering was easy compared with this.

And so the meal fell apart rather than ended and Kate was glad to reach her own room. She read her letter carefully, defending herself from the comfort of the hand-writing because just now she needed comfort so badly. They were still having a lovely time in Paris. They were sure Kate was having a lovely time in Sunny Bay. She was to remember to send the next letter to the new address in the Housing Estate so that it would be waiting for them when they moved in — ". . . that will be exciting, won't it?"

Down in the kitchen she could hear Edna and Evie clattering through the washing-up. Outside on the landing Mr. Blunt was flexing and bending. From farther off she could hear the Mad Hatter's recorder busy with a plaintive little air that said nothing that mattered, and said it very prettily.

Kate made up her mind. Somebody had to do something. She went out on to the landing, skirted the prostrate limbs of Mr. Blunt and knocked on her aunt's bedroom door. Aunt Poppy's voice invited her to come in.

Grown-up people lying in bed are always embarrassing. You know they are ill and yet they ought to be up seeing about things, oughtn't they? It's unfair. Aunt Poppy's face was pale and tired; her hair, which lay in a pigtail over one shoulder, made her look like an elderly little girl. The table beside her bed was crowded. There was a photograph of Kate's father, one she had never seen before. It must have been taken a long time ago; he looked curiously out-of-date. He had a school cap stuck on the back of his head, his hair was rising up around it like a brush, and he was grinning all over. There was a Bible on the table with texts sticking out from the pages, a tin of cough sweets, a torch, some indigestion tablets and a little pile of silver coins and some letters. None of these things were private and yet it felt as if they should have been. You wanted to look at them but when you did it made you feel nosy.

"Is that you, child?"

"How are you this morning, Aunt Poppy?"

"Just waiting for the doctor to tell me I can get up," Aunt Poppy said.

"You couldn't possibly get up, not yet."

"I can't possibly go on lying here, can I?"

Kate recognized fear in her aunt's voice, fear of what the doctor was going to say. It wasn't comfortable to be able to understand what an adult person was feeling as clearly as this.

"But if you're ill you'll have to stay in bed until you're really better."

"How can I possibly stay in bed," Aunt Poppy fretted, "with all my guests to attend to?" We're getting the words muddled, Kate thought, that's my speech — "How can I possibly stay in bed with a hockey match, an essay to write, a rehearsal for the House Play, my hair to wash?"

"But Edna and Evie are managing splendidly."

"Breakfast was all right, was it?"

"The eggs were lovely," Kate said, "and the bacon was dead right."

Aunt Poppy seemed to relax a little below the bed-clothes. "I always like people to be comfortable." The way she said it made Kate angry. It sounded servile. No-body ought to be content because the eggs for other people were lovely and the bacon was just right. "People expect to be comfortable at Sea View," Aunt Poppy said and smiled for the first time.

From the photograph on the table Kate's father

looked at her. It was her father and yet it wasn't. It was someone Aunt Poppy knew long before Kate was born, Aunt Poppy's brother, the boy who had been brought up on a farm not far from here, but who had been too clever at his books to make a farmer. She tried not to look at the photograph and gathered all the courage she had. "But if you're really ill, Aunt Poppy, you won't be able to run Sea View the way you've always run it."

"Really ill! What nonsense, child!"

"It isn't nonsense. You've been tired, you said you were tired."

"Not run Sea View? Then what should I do, I'd like to know?"

"Sell it," Kate said, "to the Hotel Splendide. That's what they want you to do, isn't it?"

"Who told you that?"

"Richard. The hotel people want it so that they can expand, don't they?"

Aunt Poppy didn't answer. Her fingers plucked at the counterpane. Kate felt frightened. The boy in the photograph was on Aunt Poppy's side.

"Things can't always go on being the same," she said. "They have to change, Aunt Poppy. You know they have."

Now it was Aunt Poppy's turn to say something. It was Aunt Poppy's turn to say how could she talk such nonsense, she didn't know anything about such things, a child like her, she should learn not to talk about things she didn't understand. It was Aunt Poppy's turn to scold her for cheek, or being nosy, or not minding her own business, or for listening to what other people said. Kate would have been glad to have been scolded for any of these things provided it put her back comfortably into the child's place and made Aunt Poppy the person who knew and understood, and did what was wise and sensible. Come on, Aunt Poppy, blow your top. But Aunt Poppy didn't, she just lay there. She raised no objections to any of the impossible things Kate had said, which meant that Kate must be right after all.

Kate had become dumb, she had nothing else to say. She moved the difficult step nearer the bed and slid her hand across her aunt's hot fingers, and knew she must go away now and that she hadn't got what she had come for.

Mr. Blunt was still there on the landing. Thump — thud, thump — thud. "Aunt — twenty — keeping — twenty-one — better — twenty-two — is — twenty-three — she?" he inquired.

"No, she isn't," Kate said loudly and rudely and went downstairs. She heard Mr. Blunt's grunt of surprise and was pleased because he had lost count and was having to start again from the beginning.

She didn't give herself time to think about what she did next. She wouldn't have been able to do it if things hadn't all been miraculously on her side, like a march-past of black cats or shooting stars. The hall was empty. Through the open door she could see the broad back of Evie, who was on her knees washing the front steps. Edna was in the dining-room laying silver and glass for lunch. There was no sign of Richard or Rose or Marni.

The Tweedles had just come downstairs; she could hear them in the lounge deciding how many rugs Mr. Tweedle was going to need. Upstairs in his room the Mad Hatter was still comforting himself with his recorder. Miss Darlington was in the porch, being quietly rapturous, which made things difficult for Evie. The door of Aunt Poppy's office lay open.

It took Kate no time at all to collect the basket with the key lying in it, no time at all to slip into the empty kitchen and collect half a loaf, a packet of butter, two eggs and a bottle of milk. These she laid in the basket, first taking the key in her free hand. Then she walked out of the back door, through the yard, bent low under the dish-cloths that were hanging crooked and still dripping after last night's rain, skirted the bushes and was now standing in front of the door in the wall. She fitted the key into the keyhole, turned it and pushed the door open. Then she stepped through it into the garden of the blind house.

This time she followed the path that led through the shrubbery. This time she came straight across the long grass without stopping to stare at the swing, the rose-drowned trellis, the sodden tennis net, the monkey puzzle. This time, instead of entering by the conservatory, she went round the house to the other side where she guessed the front door must be. Her guess was right. There it was, approached by a flight of shallow steps. She hesitated, realizing that her feet would be the first to mark the moss that had spread over every step from side to side. The moss when at last she trod on it was thick and porous like a sponge; rainwater streamed out of it, she almost slipped. At the top of the steps she had to set her basket down while with both hands she groped in the greenery that had grown right across the door. There must be a bell somewhere, or a knocker. There was no bell. She found the knocker, but had to pull sharply at it to wrench it clear of the stems of ivy. Even when she had lifted it a few inches and dropped it again the ivy deadened the sound so that it produced only a muffled clunk. And after it had fallen there was no answering sound from within the house.

The returning silence stretched itself out again. It wasn't an empty silence, it wasn't only an absence of noise. It was something positive and watchful. In spite of the thin morning sunlight which had succeeded last night's storm, Kate shivered. I can't stand here too long or I will begin to be frightened, she told herself. There is no reason why I should be frightened. I've done the polite thing. I've come to the front door and knocked. That is what front doors and knockers are for. I've come to the front door like any other visitor and I've knocked and waited. This thought afforded her a little warmth. It is always comforting to know you have been polite. How long was it, she wondered, since any other person's hand had lifted that knocker?

The warmth of good manners didn't last long. She was glad when she began to feel angry. Someone inside the house must have heard the knocker. Someone knew she was there. All right, if they weren't coming to her she would go to them. She knew the way and she had business to do. Angels of mercy expect someone to answer when they call. She seized the basket and retraced her steps to the conservatory. Once again this door was ajar. Once again, this time by herself, Kate stepped inside.

This time she allowed herself to crouch for a moment beside the weed-smothered doll's house. It was an excuse, of course, a delaying action. Once on her knees she tore at the tangled stems and was able to see into the small rooms, and to identify a pair of dolls as lifeless as their own furniture, one propped on a sofa, the other collapsed across a table where a miniature plaster ham lay ready on its cardboard plate. The plate and the ham were grey with dust.

She knew she couldn't stay with the little dolls forever. At last she stood up and looked towards the uncurtained glass door that led from the conservatory into the room beyond. This time no one was watching her from inside the room. She tried the door handle, half hoping it wouldn't turn, but it turned. She opened the door and stepped through it.

It was difficult to see the room clearly because the windows were dulled and streaked with years of wind and rain. But she knew the room was watching her; she was an intruder. The furniture, the pictures on the walls, the face of the clock, the walls themselves, the unseen spiders in their webs challenged her. What right have you to be here? You are upsetting the pattern that we have made, you are disturbing the air, you are making new sounds and new shadows. Everything that is here was chosen and used by other people long ago, everything has its place. We don't want anything to be changed. Have you been invited? Did anyone choose you? Where do you fit in?

Dust lay thick on the chairs and tables, on the mantel-piece and window-sills, and it had drawn grey lines down the folds in the curtains. There was a smell of damp and soot. In the hearth, soot covered the wreckage of a fallen nest and had spread out over the tiles. Across the carpet there was a little clearing in the dust, like a path that has been trodden by a single pair of feet crossing a field of corn. The path led to a door in the opposite wall. Apart from the soot and dust there was nothing disordered about the room. Cushions and newspapers lay ready in their places, though the papers were yellow and the cushions faded. A sheet of music rested on the open piano. Blotting-paper on the writing-desk carried the prints of the last letter that had been written there. Nothing had been finished here or brought to a conclusion. Everything had just stopped.

She crossed the room by way of the little path and reached the farther door. This took her into a large tiled hall. In the dimness a rack of coats sagged on their pegs, a dog's lead dangled. There were four doors opening from the hall. The path in the dust led her to one of them. She opened it and, as it swung, sunlight from the other side seemed to come towards her like a solid wall. It was a little while before her eyes grew accustomed to the brightness. This was a small room and it was full of sunlight from a single uncurtained window. There was a camp-bed, a table, some china piled haphazardly, a

Primus. Someone was standing at the window and had not turned when she came in.

Kate set down her basket. "I've brought you your basket," she said, and knew that her voice sounded too loud. "I don't know what you need but I've brought bread and eggs and milk and butter." The man was just a dark shape in front of the window. Outside everything was bright. This was one of the windows that Kate had seen from the far side of the bay on her first evening. There must be a good view from those windows, she had thought. It was a good view, a view of the town, the Esplanade, the pale ribbed beach, the headland beyond it, the shining curve of the waves, the dark staining seaweed. You could see everything from this window. Already on the sand families had established their encampments, deck-chairs were out. The moving specks were dogs searching for yesterday's excavations. Dogs never learn.

Still the man had not turned or spoken. He had drawn his shoulders up as if her words were hitting him. "I've brought the food myself because she's ill," Kate said. "She was taken ill last night. I don't know if it's serious but the doctor is coming again this morning and then he'll tell her." Across the room only the man's silence and stillness answered.

"You'll have to do something," she said. "You'll have to decide what to do. If she's really ill she won't be able to run Sea View much longer or look after you the way she does. She has too much to do anyway, she gets too tired. The people who own the Hotel Splendide want to buy Sea View but she wouldn't let them. If she did it would really be a good thing, because then she could re-tire. So you'd better come round and talk to her about it, when she's well enough to talk. Tomorrow would be a good time, she'll know what the doctor says by then, and she's worrying. I expect she's worrying about you. If you came tomorrow morning you could arrange things be-tween you and see what ought to be done."

If I don't keep my voice low and steady I will find that I'm shouting, Kate thought, and shouting would be frightening for both of us. "You saw me the other day," she said. "I was here with Richard — he's a boy who is staying at Sea View with his father and mother. You saw us in the conservatory; we weren't doing any harm. I suppose you thought I was nosy. I was looking at the doll's house. I used to have one when I was a little girl. I wanted to come back because there was a message in the basket for you that day. It blew away across the grass, and I picked it up and put it in my pocket because I thought it was only a grocery list — but when I looked it wasn't. It was a message from her, she'd left it in the basket for you to find. It said 'He must see you'. I wondered if it was important. I suppose it was. I think he used to live here. He told me about the swing and the monkey puzzle and the doll's house."

For a sharp scalding moment she thought the man was going to turn and speak but he did neither. If she kept on talking he wouldn't say anything, she must keep on talking. "He knew the girl the doll's house belonged to," she said. "He told me she was dead."

It was quiet enough now to hear the waves breaking. She wasn't afraid now. "Do you always stay at that window?" she asked. "Do you live in this room? What are you watching for?"

Then she didn't need any answer. "I'm sorry," she said. "I'm sorry she was drowned."

It was time for her to go. She said, "Remember, you must come tomorrow, you must do something about Aunt Poppy now that she's ill. You will come, won't you?"

At last he had turned. "What did you say?" Deaf people sometimes talk like that, they don't know how their voices sound. He repeated, "What was it you said?"

"I said you'll have to come to Sea View tomorrow and talk to Aunt Poppy."

"Who are you? What is your name?"

"Kate," she told him, "Kate Lucas," and suddenly couldn't stay any longer in the room.

✦ 8 ✦

THE TEA was rich and potent, dark brown, the colour of seaweed. They sat at the kitchen table while Edna poured out and added the milk. Then they ladled in the sugar and passed the teaspoon round. Evie brought a tin of biscuits from the shelf. "The broken ones," Edna explained. "We use them in the kitchen."

There is a friendliness about broken biscuits. They burrowed for scraps of their favourites. Marni found a piece of Neapolitan Wafer and passed it to Rose with a pleased expression, like a puppy expecting a pat on the head, but Rose ate it without even noticing. Kate had secured for herself one half of a Bourbon. She was lucky, it was the side the cream had stuck to. Catch her handing it over to anybody! She scraped the cream off in small portions with her front teeth. Marni was behaving like a loon. The clock in the hall struck half past-ten. Too early to begin expecting yet, but not too early to get ready to think about expecting.

"Just time for a quick cup before I take the coffee into the lounge," Edna said. "We always serve coffee mid-morning when it's wet. It keeps the guests sweet, that's what your aunt says."

"She's better this morning, isn't she?"

K

Edna agreed, but looked worried. "It was a nasty turn, a very nasty turn the doctor said."

"But if anybody called, any visitors I mean, she could see them, couldn't she?"

"I daresay, but the doctor says she has to stay where she is for a few days and take it easy after that. And that didn't please her. Then she's worrying about the rain; she's never happy when it rains."

"The rain isn't her fault."

Edna said: "I know, but you try telling her. And you'd be as well to keep quiet about giving me a hand with the vegetables this morning, it would only fret her. Guests are guests, that's what she says."

There was no mistake about the rain. Yesterday had been a single day of sunlight. This morning was cold and grey. There was no colour in anything, the wind was up, rain hammered against the windows and streamed down them, the doors shook, the panes rattled. If you listened you could hear the sea even from inside the house, fierce and unhappy, bored but insistent. The letters this morning were streaky and limp from the wet hand of the postman. His black cape blew up over his head as he climbed the steps.

No one had even thought of going out-of-doors. After breakfast the adults had fetched heavier cardigans and books from their bedrooms, knitting, packs of patience cards and writing-pads, and now they were in the lounge, cooped up together, not talking too much in case they ran out of things to say too early in the day. They were trying to ignore the whine of the wind, try-

142

ing to forget what a fire burning in the grate at home looked like and how comfortable their own chairs were at home, trying to avoid doing sums in their heads to work out how much money a wet day at the seaside was costing them.

Edna had accepted Kate's offer of help in the kitchen and Kate had enlisted Marni and Rose. Marni was willing enough; Rose didn't seem to care one way or another. She hadn't cared about anything very much since the evening of the thunderstorm. "It's him, Edgar," Marni explained to Kate in an aggravating know-all kind of whisper. "He knew she was staying here. He had the address and he never came."

The sliced orange discs of carrot, the shredded beans, the panful of potatoes waxy below the water were the work of the girls. Rose scraped the potatoes. Marni had objected what about her hands, but Rose said what about them and went on scraping.

"Finer than that, much finer," Edna told Kate who was busy on the carrots. "Mrs. Tweedle always looks to see if they're done fine enough for her husband. The care she takes of him, it does your heart good just to see the pair of them. Darby and Joan, if ever there was! All those years together, lovely, I call it!"

Rose shuddered and said, "They scare me stiff! They make me terrified! I try not to see them."

"Oh Rose, you thought they were funny at first. And they're only living Happily Ever After," Marni cooed, very sugary, and Rose said she knew, that was what she meant.

Evie swilled the dregs of her tea and turned the cup up in the saucer. Then she held it out to Edna. "Come on, girl, what's in the tea leaves for me?"

Marni yelped, "Oh, Edna, can you tell fortunes?"

"She can and all," Evie said. "No one like our Edna for reading the cups."

They leaned their elbows on the table and their chins on their hands. Edna studied the leaves in Evie's cup. Things weren't quite so rosy this week, she said, for a certain bearded gentleman who would be nameless except that he had a long way to go. This was because of illness, someone close but not a relative, and by the end of the week romance would be rampaging hot and sweet across Evie's path once more.

"The postman has a beard," Marni reflected, "and he has a long way to go, and Miss Lucas is ill — oh Evie!" and Evie turned pink and said talking of going she must go and count the sheets before the laundry van called. Now it was time for Marni's cup. Edna turned it between her large scrubbed fingers. "Keeping someone on the hook, are you? I wouldn't try that little game for too long, it doesn't always pay off."

"That's Mike, he was hanging around all day yesterday," Kate volunteered. "You and Rose never budged from the house. You are awful, you knew he was there."

Marni said, "Oh — him!" and of course Rose hadn't wanted to go out yesterday in case *He* came, and Kate just being tiresome said in case *Who* came, and Marni said, "You wouldn't understand." And Kate said she might if somebody gave her a clue what there was to understand about and Marni retorted if she was as thick as all that there wasn't much good explaining, and passed Rose's cup across.

"See what's in Rose's cup, Edna."

Rose protested that Edna needn't bother, she didn't believe in fortunes, and Marni said not much she didn't, she always read "The Stars and You" in the magazines, didn't she, and Rose said yes, but only for a giggle. "Well, let's giggle, it would make a nice change," Kate suggested — the heavy gloom was getting hard to stand — and Marni glowered and shushed as if Kate had said "Whoopee!" at a funeral.

There were wheels in Rose's cup, Edna said. Marni's eyes gleamed, her elbow lost no time getting busy on Rose's ribs, but Rose said so what, wheels didn't mean anything particular, what was Marni on about, and Marni said *"Wheels!"* and Rose said she wasn't deaf. These wheels weren't turning, Edna said, and Rose said somebody must have left the brakes on, then, mustn't they? News of a friend and a journey, Edna declared. Rose said the journey would be for Kate who was going home at the end of the week, the tea leaves had got into the wrong cup, and then Edna frowned and said, "Danger, there's danger!" and Rose laughed.

By this time Marni was almost frantic. Wasn't it time, she said, for Rose and her to go upstairs and do their nails, and a wet morning would be a good time for a face pack and it was two days since either of them had written their diaries, and then she gently wheeled Rose out of the room as if she'd been some kind of a prize cow that mustn't be hustled.

Kate was glad when they had gone. It was peaceable and friendly in the kitchen without them. She remembered the kitchen at home. Sometimes in the evening, while Mum was clearing up after tea, Kate went out with her skipping-rope and skipped beside the lilac tree. It was quiet at the backs of the houses. A little of the pattern of other people's lives came across the hedges; Mrs. Jamison's baby was wailing gently, the solemn boy from two doors down was practising his violin, she could hear the rhythm of Mrs. Higg's sewing-machine. The skipping-rope, as she slapped it down, made a satisfying and lonely sound. The loneliness was pleasant when you could see the light in the kitchen and hear the water running. Soon she would go in, but not until she had skipped seven times seven for luck.

When she went home at the end of the week it would be to a new kitchen in a new home. She pushed the thought out of her head and remembered that kitchens were good places for talking in. There was something she wanted to say to Edna. Things were easier to say if your hands were busy.

Edna rinsed the cups and Kate wiped. Now was the time to say it. But Edna said, "Your aunt wouldn't like it if she knew where you went with that basket yesterday."

"How do you know where I went?" Kate asked, cheeky without meaning to be, because Edna had got in first.

"I was going to take the basket myself, but butter doesn't fly nor eggs neither," Edna said. "And what did you do with the key?"

"I expect I left it in the lock. I'll go and fetch it."

"Not till the rain eases you won't."

Edna was pouring milk into the saucepan to heat for the coffee. The froth ran to the edge of the pan and gathered there. Everything Edna did was easy and accurate. Her hands knew the size and weight and feeling of things and the distances between them. Her skill was reassuring.

"Edna, I saw him yesterday. Who is he?"

"He was the gentleman your aunt was housekeeper to before she had the guest house."

"Why does he live the way he does?"

Now Edna was measuring out the coffee, spoonful by spoonful into the jug, counting inside her head. "People can choose how they live, and sometimes it's like that when a person has had a great sorrow," she said, in the important voice of someone who has more to tell.

"It was his daughter, wasn't it? The one who was drowned."

"The only daughter he had."

"How was she drowned?"

"Crossing the bay with the tide coming in."

"Surely she knew about the tide? She lived here, everybody would know."

"When you're young and in a hurry you can soon forget."

147

"Why was she in a hurry?" As long as Edna's hands were busy she would go on talking.

"They say she was coming home from school; it was the last day of her last term. She stayed talking with someone, then she came running, knowing her father would be at the window watching for her, the way he always was. The water was high, there was a storm rising."

"People must have seen."

"It can happen quick," Edna said, "when the tide's running the same way as the wind. No one could get near her, they say."

Now the lid of the kettle was stammering for attention. Edna lifted the kettle and poured the boiling water into the jug. The smell of coffee enriched the kitchen and the liquid rose in rainbow-streaked bubbles.

"Who was it she was talking to, Edna?"

"Some young fellow that lived hereabouts, so I heard," Edna said, and turned just in time to rescue the saucepan before the milk had climbed to its rim. "Her Dad didn't think much of him, the girl was all he cared about after his wife died."

"I thought the girl had a brother."

"Yes."

"What about him, then?"

Edna was setting out cups on the tray. "Him and his dad never hit it off even before. And when the girl was drowned he couldn't stand the sight of the boy, as if he grudged him for living. They say he was sent away to school, and had his holidays with friends, hardly ever home. No life that for a growing lad."

"He must be quite grown up now."

Edna agreed that he would, and distributed the teaspoons noisily in the saucers.

"Where does he live now? What does he do?"

Edna was arranging biscuits in patterns round a plate, Nice, Ginger Nut, Petit Beurre. How would she know anything about the boy, people said he'd tried one thing and another but never made a success of any of them. A drifter, that's what folk said.

"Doesn't he come back to visit his father?"

"I doubt if the old man would want to see him. He closed the doors long ago."

"But he must come back sometimes. This is his home."

"I never heard that he did," Edna said, and put two chocolate biscuits on the top to complete the pattern (perhaps Miss Darlington would be lucky this morning). "There's no one in the town would know him now except your aunt, maybe. He used to write to her. He was no more than a lad when it happened." She put the lid on the biscuit tin. The interview was over. "Go on into the lounge now. I'll be bringing in the coffee in a minute."

She found Richard in the hall. He was aiming kicks at the umbrella-stand and looked about as brisk as a cold poached egg. From the landing overhead came the vibrations of Mr. Blunt's morning activities. Kate said,

"Too wet for the pool today, anyway," because it was something to say, and it was a day or two since she'd said anything to Richard.

"Oh — that," Richard growled and landed the umbrella-stand a particularly nasty one.

"There's no need for you to go off the deep end," Kate said, and then giggled because it turned out to be funny and the wrong thing to say, and Richard asked why couldn't she go and get lost.

"I only meant it was one day less."

"Fancy being able to work that one out — fantastic!" Richard said in a grey kind of voice. "Not that it matters, anyway. Actually I went off the high board three times yesterday."

"You did?"

"I just told you I did."

"Why didn't you say before?"

"Why on earth should I?"

"Well — I expect *he* was pleased, wasn't he?" She raised her eyes in the direction of the stretch-bend-stretch that was going on above their heads. "Well, wasn't he?"

"I suppose so."

"He must have been pleased, and your mother too."

Richard didn't answer. Kate was angry and sorry for him at the same time. So yesterday's triumph hadn't come off. Poor Richard. There ought to have been brass bands and a procession, a red carpet or a loudspeaker. There hadn't been any of them. Sometimes it was like this. You heard you'd passed your exams — you'd actually passed them! — and people said, "Well of course, I knew you would," or you had the tooth out at last and no one was really interested. The slaughtered dragon had been a stuffed dragon after all.

"All the same you might have told me."

"There's no need to go on," Richard barked. "I knew I could do it, I'd done it, you saw me —"

"Yes but —"

Richard said, "Oh for any sake!" and then the girls came down the stairs. Apparently Rose had decided that face-packs and nail varnish were too much bother. Marni still wore her patient-and-loving face, but it was squarer and pinker. She looked as if she could explode at any moment.

"Edna says we're all to go into the lounge, she's bringing coffee," Kate said.

At that precise moment, mixed with the sound of the wind and the sea there came the sound of the motorbikes. First it was a long way off, no louder than a swarm of bees, then it was louder, louder still, so loud now that it swept in below the door and filled the hall and their ears. There was something terrible and lordly about the way the sound came. No other sound had a chance.

Kate looked at Rose. She was standing very still and straight. As the sound of the engines increased her face shone, like a lamp when the wick is turned up. I'm glad I'm not like her, Kate thought. I'm glad she's different. I never want to look like that — never. Marni had grabbed hold of Rose's elbow. "Listen — it's them!"

Now the sound had reached its climax. The bikes must be in front of the house. But they had not stopped, were not stopping. The sound was diminishing. It became less and less; now it had shrunk altogether, you could hear the sea again.

"They've gone past," Marni said in doom-laden tones. Rose didn't speak, but her face was small, without any hint of light.

"Those must be the chaps I saw yesterday in the Caff at the far side of the bay when I went in for a coffee," Richard said. "They've got a camp in one of the fields over there. Groovy types. You should have seen the bikes they have."

Edna appeared from the kitchen with a loaded tray. "On you go, all of you, into the lounge." The clock in the hall struck eleven as they went in. Any time, Kate thought. It could begin to happen any time.

The people in the lounge brightened at the chink of the teaspoons. They passed the cups round and made room for the girls and Richard. Mrs. Blunt went to call her husband. "How kind," they said to Edna. "How very kind."

Eleven o'clock. He will come soon. Kate had chosen a chair where without looking out she could still be aware of movement on the front steps. He'll come walking up and ring the bell and Edna will answer it, and I'll hear his voice and her voice on the porch, and his footsteps and hers going up the stairs, and Aunt Poppy's door opening and closing and Edna coming down again. I told him he must come. I told him this was the time to come. So he must come. He will come.

It used to be like this when you were little and waiting for Christmas, lying in bed staring at the darkness, trying to push yesterday into tomorrow. When you were bigger you learned that the clock went on no matter what you did. Before the clock had gone right round once —

"Well, that was a nice cup of coffee and no mistake," Mrs. Tweedle said. "We can always be sure of a good cup of coffee at Sea View, that's what we say, isn't it, William?"

Out of the corner of her eye Kate had seen a dark shape of someone walking up the steps. The bell rang and Edna answered it and the shape went down the steps again and Edna returned to the kitchen.

"The milkman, this is the day he calls for his money. Dear dear, how the days go by," Miss Darlington said. "Come and help me to wind my wool, Rose. A sweet shade, don't you think? Pink is always so warm."

Rose didn't seem to hear, but Marni said, "I'll hold it for you, Aunt Dilly!" and was soon tethered to her aunt's side, looking at Rose, hoping she would be pleased.

Rose hadn't even heard Miss Darlington's invitation. Her face had a tiptoe look that Kate recognized. So Rose was making impossible things happen, too. It wasn't a drove of motor-bikes she was hearing, it was one motor-bike coming back, one motor-bike with a purpose, slowing and stopping outside Sea View. Listen! There are footsteps coming up the steps. That's the bell. She's playing the same game as I am, Kate thought, trying like me to conjure up sounds from silence.

"At the Splendide we had films when the weather was bad," Mrs. Blunt said. "Didn't we, my dear?"

The rain redoubled its attack on the window. "Just a clearing shower," Miss Darlington said brightly.

Mrs. Blunt said, "Some of the films were really very good. Richard liked them, didn't you, Richard?"

"Far better out in the open. A little rain never did anyone any harm," Mr. Blunt said.

The Mad Hatter hadn't said anything. He was sitting with his long pale hand up against his face, pretending to read a newspaper. Perhaps he was cooking up a new joke for the afternoon Kaper but it seemed improbable. I don't think I can stand this for very much longer, Kate thought. I wish there was some way of it all stopping.

Something was coming. The laundry van drew in to the curb and the man got out. Evie took the sheets out to him, and the van drove off again.

Rose stood up and said she'd carry the cups out to the kitchen. Miss Darlington said, "Sit still, Marni, and don't wriggle. There are two more skeins to do after this."

In the hall the clock struck the half-hour.

Mrs. Tweedle produced a sheaf of photographs out of her handbag. She'd been saving these, she said, for a suitable time, and here it was, wasn't it? Nothing like snapshots to pass a few hours between friends. And more personal than films, really, didn't you think? These snapshots had been taken while Mr. and Mrs. Tweedle were staying with Mrs. Tweedle's niece at Whit. Her niece lived at Eastbourne. She and her husband had three children, dear little souls all of them, two boys and one girl. "The little girl was William's favourite, wasn't she, William?" Mrs. Tweedle said.

"It's getting in a tangle," Miss Darlington said to Marni. "Do try to sit still." Marni had an anxious eye on the door. She said mightn't it be better if Aunt Dilly put the wool round the back of one of the chairs, and Aunt Dilly said of course it wouldn't, just sit still like a good girl, and there was nothing like many hands, was there? Mr. Blunt said if it cleared up now there might just be time for a quick trot along the Esplanade and back before lunch, and Mrs. Blunt said more like a swim than a trot, and the Mad Hatter neither spoke nor moved.

I'll count up to five hundred slowly, Kate decided. I won't think about it or look, I won't wish for anything or try to make anything happen. I'll just count. It will happen while I am counting.

"Now this is my favourite, you'll like this one," Mrs. Tweedle said, putting another photograph into circulation, "William says I should send this in for one of those competitions in the magazines, don't you, William? This is William and Yvonne — Yvonne was the little girl I told you about. That's her teddy bear, one of her teddy bears. She had two, a day teddy bear and a night teddy bear, and of course we all had to remember which was which. This was the day teddy bear, isn't that right, William? Well I suppose it would be, in the middle of the afternoon. William used to tell stories for the teddy bears. And this is Justin, he's the elder of the two boys, a regular pickle he is. Very like his mother, wouldn't you say? Of course, how silly of me, you don't know my niece. Wait a moment and I'll find one of her and you can see how alike they are, Justin and his mum. She took after my sister, my sister Nell that lives in Cardiff, about the eyes, I'd say. Wouldn't you say Marianne was like Nell, William?"

"I wonder what Rose is doing," Marni said, wriggling.

"She took the cups into the kitchen for Edna," Aunt Dilly said, "and I do believe we've got another tangle, isn't that provoking? 'How all occasions do conspire against me!' as the poet sings."

"I was going to nip along to the Caff at the other side of the bay this morning if it was fine," Richard said. "I wanted to take another look at those bikes. The gang's bound to be there about now."

Two-hundred-and-twenty-one, two-hundred-and-twenty-two, two-hundred-and-twenty-three, two-hundred-and-twenty-four.

"And this is Marianne with her husband, he's called George, a nice fellow, we liked him straightaway. Actually it isn't very good of George, his ears aren't like that at all. He works in the Municipal Offices, a good safe job. That's the little pool they have in the garden, there are four goldfish in it, and they all have names. I couldn't tell one from the other but the children, they knew all right, didn't they, William?"

Three - hundred - and - seventeen, three - hundred - and - eighteen, three - hundred - and - nineteen —

In the distance a sound had separated itself from all the other sounds. It was clearer now, you could give it a name. It was the sound of a single motor-bike returning back along the Esplanade. It came nearer, very near. It stuttered, stopped. Someone came up the steps. Distantly in the kitchen a bell rang. Edna came to answer it.

Three - hundred - and - forty - one, three - hundred - and - forty - two —

Edna put her head round the door. "There's a young fellow here asking for Miss Rose," she said.

~(9)~

MISS DARLINGTON took a couple of turns of wool off the skein before she said, "Who is it, Edna?"

Edna said she hadn't asked the name. Marni, whose face already competed in brilliance with the wool that hung from her hands, said she couldn't be sure of course but perhaps it was a boy from home called Edgar. Rose had said something about Edgar coming to camp somewhere around; she thought Rose might have told him where she was staying.

"From home, is he?" Miss Darlington said. "Do be careful what you're doing with the wool, Marni." She said perhaps Edna had better go and tell Rose the boy was here and ask her to go and see what it was he wanted. "She's out in the kitchen, isn't she?"

"No, I thought she was here, that's why I came." Edna sounded impatient, her mind was on her waiting saucepans.

"But surely she took the cups out to you, didn't she?"

"That was a while back. She isn't in the kitchen now."

"Then she must be up in her room," Miss Darlington decided and wound the final lap of wool on to her ball with a little flourish. "Run upstairs, Marni, and tell

Rose to come down. I expect Edna's busy with the lunch just now, aren't you, Edna? I know you don't like lunch to be late."

Marni was off like an arrow from a bow and came back again in a few moments. Messengers in Shakespearean plays arrived, catapulted from the wings, with faces as important as Marni's was now. Rose wasn't in her room, she reported, and she had looked out of the window and it was Edgar who was waiting right enough. So what was she to do?

With infuriating patience Miss Darlington's nails picked at a knot in her wool. "Just tell the boy Rose isn't here, dear, and then come back straightaway so that we can start another skein."

Marni didn't budge. Her face was square, mules had nothing on her. "Run along now," her aunt urged. "If it's anything important you can always take a message, can't you?" Just ask the silver-tongued Hermes to state his business, tell the Angel Gabriel nothing today, thank you.

"She must be somewhere in the house," Marni persisted.

"I thought you said you'd looked."

"I have, but —"

"Where have you looked?"

"She isn't in the kitchen, she isn't up in our room —"

"That young boy won't like being kept waiting in all this rain," Miss Darlington said. "Off you go and tell him what I said."

Marni glowered and held her ground.

"She would hardly have gone out, would she?" Mrs. Blunt inquired.

"That's it, she's gone out for an airing," Mr. Blunt decided. "Wise girl, getting up an appetite for her lunch, just what we should all be doing!"

The gale beat in fresh frenzy on the window-pane. The window was seized and shaken — water streamed down it, turning everything in the street into liquid objects that had no names or shape.

"I'm sure the child has more sense than to go out in that weather," Mrs. Tweedle said. "She'd be soaked through to the skin in no time at all."

"Through to the skin," Mr. Tweedle agreed.

"She could pick up pneumonia out on a day like that," Mrs. Tweedle declared. "It could go right to the chest."

"To the chest as easy as winking," said Mr. Tweedle.

"Young people don't think, some of them."

"They're young. They don't think."

Last term the Upper Sixth had done a Greek play in which the Chorus had gone on at each other like this for hours — "Woe, woe!" "Alas, alas!" Kate and Hazel had made themselves sore trying not to laugh out loud. But just now it wasn't funny.

"In any case," Mrs. Blunt said, "where would she want to go?"

"That's right," Aunt Dilly agreed, as if the habit of winding wool had infected her so that she could now only reason in circles. "Where indeed, that's what I say. And that boy out there is getting wetter every minute. Perhaps Rose is in Kate's room."

Marni declared that she had looked in Kate's room, and Rose wasn't there either.

At this moment the clock in the hall struck midday. It was the firmness and purpose of the twelve strokes that released Kate from this goldfish bowl where everything went round and round and nothing happened. What was the good of waiting and hoping, what was the sense of expecting yourself silly? She'd had enough. She'd *make* things happen.

Probably no one noticed her as she left the lounge. She snatched a quick glance through the open door and across the porch. Even helmeted and muffled, Edgar was still magnificent. Evie was washing coffee-cups at the sink and didn't turn as Kate skimmed through the kitchen and out from the back door. What was the sense of wasting time with coats or hoods?

She had to fight with the wind before she was able to pull the door closed behind her. Dish-cloths whipped her forehead as she ran below them, the bushes reached out drenched arms at her, pieces of leaf and twig dislodged by the gale blew into her hair and eyes and were washed away again by the next onslaught of the rain. Now she had come to the door in the wall; her fingers sought for and found the key in the lock. Both the lock and her fingers were slippery. As soon as she had succeeded in turning the key the storm caught the door and flung it open in front of her. This time she knew there was no hope of closing it; she left it swinging behind her and followed the path to the house.

When she was clear of the shrubbery she was at once exposed to the full fury of the wind. Here the sagging rose trellis rocked and creaked like a struggling animal, the seat of the swing moved as if someone had lately risen from it. The ungainly branches of the monkey puzzle swayed in a confused pattern of darkness. And all the time the voice of the sea grew stronger and clearer. Kate had never heard it like this, not even on the night of the thunderstorm.

She was forced to bend low and fight for breath as she covered the short distance to the conservatory door. Now at last she had gained a little respite from the wind; she could breath more easily. Now if she reached out she would be able to push the door open and step into shelter, into dry calm air.

Her hand had found the door but when she pushed it it did not yield. She pushed again with more vigour, lost her balance and blundered sideways into a pool where water had gathered at the bottom of a gushing downspout. The coldness and shock made her gasp, the legs of her jeans were soaked. Come on, come on — open up! Although in her heart she knew it would be useless she tried the door once more — but still it wouldn't budge. Inside she could see the doll's house, safe and still, dry and dusty, taking no damage from the gale. But the door between them was locked; this time she could not get in.

But she had to get in. She must get in. Gasping and stumbling, using her hands more than her eyes, she worked her way round the house to the front door and beyond it, making for the one window where she knew she could demand entrance. Here on the seaward side the thunder of the breaking tide was louder still, shutting out even the scream of the wind, filling everything with its own rhythm, its plunge and suck and sigh.

As soon as she reached the window she could see his face appearing as a pale shape on the other side of the glass. He didn't see her, all his attention was focussed on the beach below and beyond her. Even when she stood upright and called to him he didn't appear at first to hear her. She had to come close against the pane, to beat with spread palms on the glass and shout, "Let me in! Let me in!"

He had seen her now and was staring. She knew he recognized her and for a moment she thought he was going to turn away. Once again, louder this time, she called, "Let me in! You must let me in!" Then his hand beckoned her to a small door at the farther side of the window. She stumbled towards it and stood waiting. She heard bolts scrape and a key turn and then the door swung open. At last she was inside the house.

When he had closed the door behind her she found that her ears were singing, and it was a moment or two before she was able to speak. Now the sound of the storm was more remote, and inside the room there was nothing to be heard except her own quick breathing and the rainwater dropping from her clothes. The dry stale air of the house caught at her throat.

The man hadn't spoken either, he was still looking past her shoulder into the bay. At last Kate found breath and the words she needed.

"You should have come this morning, I told you you ought to come. I told you what would be the best time and I waited, all morning I've been waiting. If you weren't going to come you might have told me so yesterday. Edna says the doctor's worried about her; he says she must stop working the way she does. If you'd come and talked it would have done her good. If *you'd* been ill she would have come, wouldn't she? Oh yes, but that would have been different! You don't object to her doing your errands and your laundry because she's a servant, she's always been a servant, she's looked after you all these years. If it hadn't been for her you couldn't have shut yourself up the way you have, could you? You wouldn't have been able to walk out on everything! And if it hadn't been for you she wouldn't be ill now and worried and too tired all the time. She could have sold the guest house a long time ago — I told you — and have enough money to stop working. I'll tell you something you don't know. She's going to have to stop working soon — because she hasn't enough help, and the place is getting shabbier and shabbier over there, no matter how hard she tries, and people only go there now because she's kind or because they can't afford to stay anywhere better. Some summer soon nobody will want to stay there — then what will you do?"

She had never intended to speak like this and her own voice frightened her, but there was now no way of stopping. In any case she didn't think her words meant anything to him; nothing she said was reaching him, she might as well not have said it. Nothing was real or mattered to him except the army of the incoming waves riding up into the bay.

She turned to look in the direction where he was looking. She had never seen the bay like this before. Though the sky was low and packed densely with clouds, the bay seemed to be filled with moving light, the light of tormented water, wave after wave crowding up the beach, hurling against the crescent border of tame sand that was still visible along the edge. It was impossible to believe that yesterday the bay had held a litter of deck-chairs and sandcastles, prams, thermos flasks and babies, dogs and knitting-baskets, and that a dozen transistor sets had drowned the gently-lapping water. That must have happened in another world.

She would make him listen to what she had come to say. "I know about her, I know she was drowned there in the bay. I know why you shut yourself away from other people and won't let yourself think about anything but her. That's what you've done, isn't it, making sure nobody else matters to you and you don't matter to anybody. At least that's what you think you've done — but you haven't. And I suppose you think it was something big. What about Aunt Poppy? What about her? She has to stay here so that she can look after you and protect you from all the things outside, and now she's ill and worried and you aren't bothering to go and discuss with her what is the best thing to do. And what about him — the girl's brother? It wasn't his fault he wasn't the one who was drowned. Do you know about him, what he's doing? I'll tell you. He's being the funny man in a crummy Concert Party at the far end of the Esplanade — we saw him, being funny in the afternoon and funny again in the evening while he waits to get a message from you to say you want to see him, and he is to come home."

She thought perhaps the man was hearing her now but she couldn't be sure. She was shocked at herself for having spoken like this, for having enjoyed it, for having enjoyed the power the words gave her. She came closer and stood beside him.

"Listen," she said, more gently. "Things that have happened have happened, no matter how terrible and sad they are, but there are still all the other people, you have to live in the world with them. And if you do, it doesn't mean any —" she fumbled for the word, it was important to find the right one — "any — disrespect for the people who have died." It wasn't the right word but it would have to do.

Suddenly the man's hand reached for her wrist and held it so tightly that it hurt. "Down there," he said. "Look! Look — there she is!"

His other hand was pointing down towards the bay. At first she could see no one. "There!" he repeated. "There!"

Now she could see. Away at the far end of the bay,

where the promontory was visible only because of the great columns of spray shooting up from the rocks, something was moving, was coming in this direction, was crossing the bay at the fringe of the oncoming water. If it hadn't been for the vivid orange sweater no one would have known that anything human was on the beach or could have identified the figure. Rose, it was Rose! She must have gone across to the Caff where Richard had said the boys from the camp called in each morning. Now she was coming back, the quick way.

Her wrist was smarting. Kate tried to pull it free. "Can't you see?" the man demanded.

"Yes, but she'll be all right. She knows about the tide. She's careful."

"Being careful won't help her on a day like this," the man said.

"But the water never comes as far up as that, everyone knows it doesn't." There was always below the wall of the Esplanade a few yards of white dry sand that the sea never reached — deep desert sand, the Sahara, the children called it. They enjoyed running up from the firm sand below and racing into the Sahara at full speed, discovering how far they could go until their feet sank up to the ankles and they were brought to a standstill. Boys riding their bicycles competed with each other to reach the wall before the tyres were buried and they fell off.

"With a tide and a wind driving together," the man said, "the waves will be against the sea-wall in no time at all — over the wall."

"She'll be across the bay before it comes as close as that."

"I tell you she's cutting it too fine."

"That means she'll be here all the sooner."

"Listen," the man said, "I know. I've seen it."

She couldn't argue, there was no sense in arguing, she knew that what he said was true. The bright speck of colour down on the shore was nearer but there was still a long way to come. Kate remembered the evening when she had crossed the bay with Richard, and how when the tide had turned it seemed as if the whole beach tilted and the mass of water came sliding towards them.

"I'll go," she said. "I'll tell them."

Thinking about it afterwards she didn't remember the journey back from the blind house across the garden and along the path through the shrubbery. She remembered being grateful that the door in the wall was open and swinging on its hinges so that no moments were lost, she remembered Edna's startled face looking up from a saucepan. "Where in all the world —?" But she didn't wait to answer. As she came through the hall she saw that the porch was now empty.

There they were in the lounge, just as she had left them, as if they had got caught in some kind of a boring game and didn't know how to bring it to a conclusion. Marni was tethered to a new skein of wool, Miss Darlington's hands might never had stopped moving, the Mad Hatter hadn't budged from his unhappy private world, Mr. and Mrs. Tweedle dozed and dreamed harmoniously of the lunch they hoped to eat in half an hour. Mrs. Blunt played with a magazine. It was obvious from their faces that Mr. Blunt and Richard had found nothing new to say to each other.

Miss Darlington looked up as Kate burst through the door. Her eyes widened, her hands slowed and stopped. "Kate!"

Kate said: "It's Rose! You have to come!"

"Rose?"

"Please come!"

"What do you mean? Where is Rose? Where have you been to get yourself in such a state?"

She explained, throwing the explanation at them between her own fight for breath. She had seen Rose at the far side of the bay. Now Rose was coming back, she was crossing in front of the tide, the wind was driving the water high up the beach, Rose might not know how high, she could be trapped trying to take the short-cut.

"Oh, the stupid girl," Aunt Dilly said. "Surely she ought to realize —" but the Mad Hatter uncoiled and was on his feet. "Kate's right," he said, "no time to lose." He turned to Mr. Blunt. "We must get down there right away. And you, Richard, you come too."

It took a few minutes to reach the Esplanade — they had to struggle against the wind all the way. Streets and pavements were deserted. Kate, Richard and Marni arrived at the sea-wall only moments behind the Mad Hatter and Mr. Blunt. Somewhere in the rear Mrs. Blunt and Aunt Dilly could be heard noisily encouraging each other along.

Though it was probably less than five minutes since

Kate had looked out from the window of the blind house, the scene had changed significantly. The waves already had advanced to the edge of the dry sand of the Sahara and were still advancing. The air was full not only of rain but of salt sea spray, so that their faces stung and their vision was dimmed. Where was Rose? How far had she come? How far had she still to come?

"There she is! There!"

It didn't seem to Kate that Rose had made much progress. It was easy to understand why. Already she wasn't running on sand but in the swirling border of the water. Sometimes it was up to her ankles; sometimes a wave reached to her knees, sometimes above them.

"Why doesn't she come in towards the sea-wall?"

"She can't see! She can't see!"

Rose's hands were up at her eyes, knuckling them free from rain and sea-water. Her pace had slowed — a wave knocked her off balance so that she staggered. If she had turned shoreward sooner she would have reached the foot of one of the flights of steps that ran from the ter-race of the Esplanade down to the level of the beach, but she had gone past one of these flights — perhaps she hadn't been able to see it — and the next was some dis-tance ahead of her.

"Get the life belt, quick!"

There were several life-belts which hung with ropes looped from pegs on the wall of the terrace between urns of geraniums. They had all seen them every day, tidy, intriguing, official objects. Where was the nearest life belt hanging — this way or farther on?

"Look! Look! She's reached the rocks!"

Rose had come to the cluster of great smooth black rocks halfway along the beach. She was keeping close to the rocks, perhaps in the hope of gaining a little shelter. The breakers had reached the rocks before her and were already swirling round them, reaching out to join forces on the shoreward side. Water was thrown up into the air and for a moment the watchers lost sight of the orange sweater altogether.

"She's getting more shelter now," Kate said, and heard Richard's half-moan in answer. "Fool! Fool! Can't you see? She's forgotten about the pools!"

At the base of the rocks the incoming tides had scooped out hollows where, even in fine weather, pools lay, pools that were warm and smooth and safe enough for young children to paddle in, pools that gave them a couple of yards of peaceful water in which to splash under the admiring eyes of mums and grannies. Now the breakers had filled these pools and it was impossible to see that they were there.

Rose was growing tired. As she came close to one of the rocks they saw that she reached out a hand to touch it, as if its solidity gave her a kind of comfort. But Richard was right, she had forgotten the pools were there. She had stumbled into one of them, had lost her footing, had fallen, was waist deep and trying to rise. Now she was down in the water again as another wave overtook her. Kate heard her own voice shouting, "Rose! Rose!"

Mr. Blunt had run for the life-belt, they could hear him coming back though no one looked in his direction

since they were all staring into the water where sometimes Rose was visible, where sometimes she was hidden.
It seemed to them that she had found her feet, but always the next crest of water knocked her down again and
ran over her head.

Mr. Blunt and the Mad Hatter were fumbling with the
coil of line. It had tangled — they had been in too much
of a hurry. At last they had the life-belt free and ready to
throw. But even as it swung in Mr. Blunt's hands the
gale blew it back towards him. Against this wind it could
travel no distance. "It's too heavy."

"Here — give me the end of the line. I'll take it."

Richard had seized the free end of the line before
either of the men had realized what he was doing or
could argue. Holding it, he had gone off the sea-wall into
a flurry of wind and spray and seething water. Sometimes they could see where he was, sometimes they lost
sight of him and only knew from the jerking line that he
was there.

"He'll make it," Mr. Blunt said. "He's going to make
it." His hands held the coil, paying the line out foot by
foot. The Mad Hatter was already over the sea-wall and
in the water, fighting his way towards Rose and the boy.

All her life Kate would remember the moment when
they knew that Richard had got there, when the line
tightened and steadied, when Mr. Blunt's hands began
slowly to pull it in. She would remember the Mad Hatter with water round his shoulders stretching out to
Rose and reaching her, Rose's hair floating in the tide,
Richard swimming like a dog, the Mad Hatter's hand

crooked at last over the top of the wall, Rose's face as Mr. Blunt stooped down to lift her across it. That picture of the drowned Ophelia, it was right after all. She was beautiful. Kate would remember Marni crying out loud, Richard crouched beside his father, holding his stomach and heaving out sea-water, and Mr. Blunt's face; and the faces of Mrs. Blunt and Miss Darlington, with Edna hard on their heels, arriving on the scene when it was all over, when Rose was safe, when the waves which had stormed right across the Sahara and were hammering the sea-wall could not touch her.

"We've done it," Mr. Blunt was saying over and over again to nobody in particular. "We've done it. We've done it. We've done it."

The Mad Hatter, water pouring from his clothes, gripped the top of the wall and stood with his head down, gasping and spitting, his shoulders heaving. Then someone said, "Look! Look — who is it? That old gentleman, who is he? Over there — look!" and pointed.

The Mad Hatter straightened up and tried to wipe the water from his eyes with his dripping sleeve. Now they were all staring towards the short slope of scrubby sandhills which separated the grounds of the blind house from the beach. Across these sandhills a man was coming. He tried to run but he stumbled, hesitated, steadied himself and came on. Sometimes he paused to shade his eyes as if they couldn't bear the light, then with his hands stretched out in front of him took a few more uncertain steps. But there was nothing uncertain about the Mad Hatter as he went forward to meet him.

M

Lunch at Sea View, in spite of Edna's well-laid plans, wasn't over until four o'clock that afternoon. The kitchen and the bathroom were crammed with steaming garments. Rose was upstairs in her bed, full of hot soup and comfort. Nobody at table grumbled. Nobody talked very much. Nobody thought of apologizing for giving trouble or for being late. "For these and all Thy mercies," Mr. and Mrs. Tweedle said when the meal was over, and this time there was no doubt about the "Amen".

Kate wanted to speak to Richard, but she didn't have a chance. He went straight upstairs between his father and mother; the door was closed before she reached the landing. Families were like that, you couldn't blame them, they had the right sometimes to shut other people out.

The Mad Hatter was coming downstairs carrying a suitcase. "Moving house," he said briefly as he met Kate. "Going home. Tell your aunt I'll be back later and let her know how things are."

"I want to ask you something," Kate said.

"Well?"

"Was it my father that she was talking to the day she was drowned crossing the bay?"

"Yes," he told her, "it was your father."

"How old was he?"

"They were both fifteen."

"Rose is fifteen," she said.

"Yes."

She said, "Thank you for telling me."

There was no sign of Marni. Miss Darlington was on

the upper landing; she had just come out of Rose's room. Her face was pink and she was crying softly and happily, but for once she seemed to have nothing at all to say.

Kate reached her own room and lay on the bed, staring at the ceiling with whose cracks she was now perfectly familiar. She was tired. Even her bones were tired.

She remembered that she hadn't written the letter she knew she ought to write. Tomorrow they would be arriving home at the new house in the Housing Estate.

She was much too tired now to write any letter, she would have to wait until her head stopped whirling and she had got her thoughts sorted out, until a kind of ordinariness had returned to this extraordinary afternoon. But yesterday she had bought a postcard, intending to send it to Hazel. It was a picture of Sunny Bay at its sunny best on a sunny evening. It showed the crescent beach, the Esplanade, the bandstand, the coloured lights, the small creamy waves, the geraniums in their urns, the moon in a calm sky.

She addressed the card to Mr. and Mrs. Godfrey Pennington and wrote the new address underneath for the first time. Then she wrote: "Welcome home. Love from Kate."

The wind had fallen and the rain was over. There was even a hint of a watery sun. She must go out soon and post the card so that it would arrive tomorrow. Better late than never. Five words weren't very much, but this time she felt that she had found the right words for the job.

﹏❨ 10 ❩﹏

FROM THE VERY MOMENT of waking she knew that this
was the last day, the day she was going home. Even before her eyes were open, while she was still nuzzled into
the pillow, the morning at Sea View Guest House, the
last morning, was all round her, like a dress that she had
put on, a dress that fitted her now, a friendly dress.

That was the kitchen radio perky and companionable,
there was Edna busy with the dustbins, now the cat rattled its breakfast saucer. Outside Kate's door someone
crossed the landing and she heard the triumphant bolt
shot across the bathroom door — bet you that was Miss
Darlington, she always made a drama out of pouncing
into the bathroom before other people. This morning the
sound of the sea had shrunk to a whisper, soft and regular as breathing. Starlings chatted briskly from the
bushes and from overhead came the lofty voices of the
seagulls travelling high across the roof-tops to explore the
sand that last night's tide had prepared for them. Now
Kate could hear the stealthy prancing of Mr. Blunt's pre-
breakfast exercises. It was not surprising so many fish
bones showed through the pattern on Aunt Poppy's carpet. This morning there was no tune from the Mad Hatter's recorder — he had been sleeping at the blind house

ever since the storm on the seashore. Perhaps it was from his room that Kate last night had noticed a window shining, a surprised golden square where she had never seen a light before.

Happily she lay, collecting the sounds and putting names to them, and when she rolled onto her back and opened her eyes there was the sunlight on the ceiling, bright and shining. Tomorrow the same sun would shine across a different ceiling, a ceiling she didn't know yet but would have to learn.

It was no use imagining what the new house would be like — anyway she knew what it would be like, didn't she? Mr. Pennington had driven Mum and Kate over to look at it one Sunday a couple of months ago. Mum and Mr. Pennington had walked round the rooms and up and down stairs measuring things and calling to each other and writing figures down in their notebooks. The sofa would fit in here, the bookcase would have to go across the other wall, the curtains would need to be let down or wouldn't it be better to have new curtains? Their footsteps and voices sounded very loud, not like indoor noises at all. The rooms smelled of putty and paint and plaster and wood, and the windows had white blobs daubed on the glass. None of it seemed to Kate to be real, it was a game they were playing; she used to play house with Hazel ages and ages ago, but on this Sunday afternoon she didn't feel in the mood to pretend. She hoped it would soon be time to go back to the old house for tea and that Mum would allow her to make toffee on the stove afterwards. Making toffee is a comfortable operation and is part of a pattern. Things ought to be part of a pattern. How could the sofa be anywhere else than where it had always been?

"This is your room, Kate. You'll have plenty of space here for all your belongings, won't you?"

"Yes."

"Where will you put your pictures?"

"I don't know yet."

"And there are going to be some fitted shelves to take your books."

"Oh."

"You'll have a good view from the window, won't you?"

A view of gardens half made and houses half built, lorries, ladders and a bulldozer. But who will watch the procession of swans coming up the canal, solemn white birds on slow grey water? Do you remember the year the canal froze right over and the swans were left with only a small patch of water to live in until the ice melted? We went down to the bottom of the garden and threw bread out to them, do you remember? And they came out on to the ice, waddling, with their pink feet turned in and greedy necks stretching.

In some ways Kate was glad this was the last morning at Sea View. Things had been different since that day of the rescue on the shore. People had been different too. Once the danger was over they seemed to grow apart from each other, as if they felt safer with their lives buttoned up into families or relationships. The Blunts were always together now, and Mrs. Blunt had stopped complaining. The Mad Hatter came and went between the blind house and Sea View and he seemed to be quite sure about everything he was doing and didn't need to make jokes to help himself along. Aunt Poppy was getting better quickly now; the doctor was pleased with her progress. She had long private talks with the Mad Hatter. The old gentleman from the blind house hadn't come to see her yet; his father was tired with all the excitement, the Mad Hatter reported; he would come when he was rested. Marni was out most of the time with Mike. Kate had seen them swinging hands along the Esplanade and on the beach and in the ice cream shop. They didn't seem to have found much to talk about yet, but it didn't appear to matter.

Rose was the most puzzling of all. Kate had expected she would look different, or heroic, but she looked just the same and didn't go out much or seem inclined to talk. She wound wool for her aunt and painted her nails a new colour and sometimes she did jigsaws. Edgar hadn't called again. Yesterday evening when they were all in the lounge and Rose was doing a jigsaw the motor-bikes came past, roaring, majestic as an army, so that the window-frames shook. "Those boys," Mr. Tweedle grumbled. "They're only young, William," Mrs. Tweedle said, and Mr. Tweedle said "Yes, I know," and went back rather sadly to his book.

Rose must have heard the bikes. She must have heard them. Aunt Dilly was trying to help her with the jigsaw, and was being enthusiastic and tiresome, seizing pieces and putting them in all the wrong places. Above the noise of the bikes Rose said, "Not there, Aunt Dilly." She took the piece out of Miss Darlington's hand and fitted it smoothly into the puzzle lower down. "It goes there!" It was as difficult as ever to guess what Rose felt or how much she minded about things or how frightened she had been. Like the ice on the canal, something had frozen up. She'd done her hair a new way, too. She'd told Marni she'd been alone to the Caff at the far side of the bay that morning, but when she got there there was no sign of Edgar and she was coming back quickly without looking very much and the rain got into her eyes so that she didn't see the tide coming in. That was all she'd said, Marni reported to Kate. After that there hadn't been a word. "Rose is like that sometimes," Marni said.

Kate on this last morning dressed quickly in shorts and jersey. She had planned it yesterday, she wanted to be there and back before breakfast. It was to be a small private celebration of goodbye, a way of remembering, like sticking photographs into an album. It was something she wanted to do by herself, unhampered by all the other people.

The morning smelled new and salty. Evie must have been up early washing the front steps — they were drying slowly in white patches. Kate jumped clean across them, and was soon out on the pavement and moving towards the Esplanade. Few people were about. A boy went from door to door sticking folded newspapers into letter-boxes. A shopkeeper polished his window. Cats waited patiently to be let in. White plumes of smoke rose from some of the chimneys.

She ran down the first flight of steps and shed her sandals as soon as she reached the firm sand. Last night's tide had left the beach rippled, there were no other marks on it except the marks of seagulls' feet, like giant embroidery stitches. Here and there seaweed was spread, delicate green hairs or bunches of thick brown ribbons. There were shells, clean-washed and shining, not touched by anyone since the receding water had left them there.

The sea was glassy smooth. At its edge wrinkles gathered and became small waves which, when Kate least expected it, collapsed in a startling way and slid back without any fuss at all to make room for other waves. Though the water was clear it seemed heavy, she had to pull her feet through it. How cold it was! She stood on tiptoe as it crept further up and reached the back of her knees. Below her feet she felt the ribs in the sand, which this quiet tide had not yet disturbed.

When she had waded out as far as was possible she looked back at the waking town, at the shapes and colours of the roofs and houses, at the breakfast smoke, and then across to the promontory on the far side of the beach. This was the pattern of Sunny Bay. She intended to remember it and take it with her. Inland a dog barked, a milk lorry rumbled. This was how the day's pattern began.

She looked across at the blind house, and though it was too far away to be certain she thought that at some of the upstairs windows the curtains had been drawn back. Today's sun would be able to travel round the wallpaper.

She remembered the doll's house and the thought frightened her. Nothing at all happened inside the doll's house, no sun, no waking, no steps, no voices, no doors opening and shutting. The dolls had not moved. The ham still waited on its cardboard plate.

Someone was calling to her. It was Peter. She hadn't seen him since the night of the fireworks. He was walking along the edge of the water scudding little flakes of flat stone. There was no good trying to get away, she couldn't move quickly with the water lapping her knees.

He said, "I thought it was you," and she said, "Well, it is," and felt foolish, waiting for him to go away, but he didn't.

He said, "I haven't seen you since that night at the fireworks," and she stooped a little and stirred the water with the tips of her fingers as if she hadn't heard.

"You look different."

She thought she owed him some kind of an explanation, so she said: "It's my face. Rose had been doing things to it that night. That was why I looked so peculiar."

"You didn't look peculiar."

"Oh, I did."

She waited for him to tell her about a cousin of his who did things to her face and how peculiar she looked, but he didn't. Four separate small waves deposited themselves at his feet, making miniature thunder.

"I'm going home this morning."

"Are you? Will you be coming back next year?"

"I don't know. Will you?"

"I don't know."

She waited for him to tell her where he might be going next year if he didn't come to Sunny Bay, but he was dumb.

"Why don't you think you'll be coming here?"

"Oh, I don't know," she said, flicking the surface of the water with her finger and thumb. It made a satisfying "plonk" and a jet of bright water shot through the air and fell.

"Would you like to come back?" he asked.

"I don't know. It depends. Things aren't ever the same anyway, are they?"

She dredged for and caught a juicy piece of brown seaweed and flourished it like a banner round her head so that drops fell from it in a silver circle.

"All sorts of things can happen in a year," she said, and waited for him to predict what was likely to happen to him, but he offered no guesses. Whatever happened to either of them, Kate thought, the tides in Sunny Bay would still be coming in and going out.

She waded clear of the water. "I've got to go back or I'll be late for breakfast."

He held out a handful of shells. "I've been collecting these. You can take your pick, if you like."

She chose the best of them, fat, curved and shiny, faintly pink. "You can put it on your mantelpiece," he suggested. Now he would tell her all the things he had on his mantelpiece and why they were there. No. He didn't.

"Goodbye," she said.

"Goodbye."

The man who looked after the deck-chairs was taking down the boards round his hut and stacking the chairs ready for the visitors when they came to claim them. It was going to be hot today. There would be plenty of visitors; the beach would be crowded. When the chairs went back again into the hut Kate would still be on the train.

She ran all the way back to Sea View. The fish cart had stopped outside the door. Evie was out with a white tray propped on her hip, choosing fish. The postman had come past and was helping her to choose. The silver fish swung from his fingers and flopped on to the tray. To-night at Sea View there would be fish for supper.

After breakfast there was time to pack and to visit Aunt Poppy, who was propped up in bed and looked almost well again.

"Give my love to your mother," Aunt Poppy said.

"Yes, I will."

"Tell her I'll be writing soon. Tell her there may be changes here."

"Yes, Aunt Poppy."

"Tell her I hope she will be very happy."

She kissed Aunt Poppy goodbye and said goodbye to the photograph of the smiling boy in the school cap.

"How old was he when that was taken?"

"Fifteen," Aunt Poppy told her. "That was a long time ago."

Edna came to say the car was at the door to take Kate to the station. Kate went upstairs and brought her case. Each step on the way down was a kind of goodbye.

There were more goodbyes waiting for her. They were there in the hall and in the porch and gathered on the steps. Richard was there and Mr. Blunt and Mrs. Blunt, Edna and Evie and even the postman on his way back to the post office with an empty bag, Marni, Rose and Miss Darlington, Mr. and Mrs. Tweedle. The Mad Hatter was holding something in his hands, a little box.

"He wanted you to have them. He said you were to take them with you," he said.

Kate lifted the lid and saw the little dolls from the doll's house. She closed the lid quickly and was going to protest, "I'm too old for dolls," when the Mad Hatter said, "A change of scenery, don't you know," and smiled, so she said "Thank you — oh thank you!" and got into the car.

They stood there smiling as the car drove off, lined up and already slightly unreal, like a photograph. Kate leaned out and waved to them as long as she could see them.